Victorious Christian Faith

By Alan Redpath:

VICTORIOUS CHRISTIAN LIVING
VICTORIOUS PRAYING
VICTORIOUS CHRISTIAN SERVICE
THE ROYAL ROUTE TO HEAVEN
THE MAKING OF A MAN OF GOD
BLESSINGS OUT OF BUFFETINGS
FAITH FOR THE TIMES
LAW AND LIBERTY
VICTORIOUS CHRISTIAN FAITH

Victorious Christian Faith

Alan Redpath

Fleming H. Revell Company
Old Tappan, New Jersey

Library of Congress Cataloging in Publication Data

Redpath, Alan
Victorious Christian faith.

1. Christian Life—1960–   . I. Title.
BV4501.2.R423   1984   248.4   84-4719
ISBN 0-8007-1208-0

Contents

Introduction

It hardly seems necessary to introduce my good friend Alan Redpath. Few men in our time are so widely known, loved, and read as he is. At the same time, I welcome this opportunity to commend him and his latest book, *Victorious Christian Faith,* to a younger readership who may not be familiar with his name. I feel somewhat qualified to do so, since my association with this man of God spans some forty years of my ministry—and that is a long time! During this period, our oneness in life, love and service in Christ has been something special. I would not trade anything for the competition on the golf course, the comradeship in the ministry—including evangelistic crusades, Christian Life Conventions, exchange of pulpits—the conversations in times of crises and calm, and above all, the communion with heaven when together we've knelt to conquer.

This stunning book, therefore, is what I would expect of Alan Redpath. It is the man in action, glorifying his Lord instead of advertising himself. It is Alan Redpath spelling out both the truth and terms of "full salvation" in Christ. The truth is Jesus Christ crucified, risen, living, and coming again. The terms are repentance, faith, obedience, discipline, and maturity—made real in us through the cross, the Word, and the Spirit. He himself says, "I make no apology for using such words as *discipleship, discipline,* and *obedience* over and over, because that is what Christian living is all about."

Victorious Christian Faith is personal in its style, especially the Preface, Prologue, and Epilogue. Indeed, the reader will be deeply moved by Dr. Redpath's story of the illness that threatened to take his life and to terminate his ministry in 1964. I recall seeing him shortly after his stroke, during a city-wide crusade in Edinburgh, Scotland, in 1965. The evangelistic effort was his idea in the first place. He saw the vision and sensed the burden to reach men and women with the Gospel. In the midst of the preparations, he was struck down. Learning of this, I took steps to cancel the crusade, but Redpath's immediate response was, "No way! You are coming. The crusade is on." And for three solid weeks that dear man, with impaired speech and body partially paralyzed, oversaw the counseling night by night. Small wonder, then, that God worked in such power and blessing! The personal style of the book, however, carries over to the rest of the chapters. As far as he is concerned, "there is always more to experience . . . no one has arrived." His life text is J. B. Phillips' rendering of Philippians 4:13, "I am ready for anything through the strength of the One who lives within me." This comes through repeatedly as you peruse the pages.

The book is also practical in its scope. While biblical truth saturates its message, the intention of the author is not so much to educate as to activate the believer. He sums it up when he writes: "It's not more doctrine that we need, but 100 percent obedience to what we know."

Victorious Christian Faith is mainly pastoral in its strength. The book throbs with the passion and purpose of a true pastor: to preach Christ, ". . . warning every man, and teaching every man in all wisdom; that . . . [he might] present every man perfect in Christ Jesus" (Colossians 1:28). Nothing less than reaching the summit of victorious faith is the dominating theme. The mountaineer must *climb.* He must ". . . press on toward the goal to win the prize . . ." (Philippians 3:14 NIV). The mountaineer must *cling.* The steeper the climb, the tighter he must hold on. It was Barnabas who exhorted the young converts at Antioch to ". . . cling unto the Lord. . . . with purpose of heart . . ." (Acts 11:23 NEW SCOFIELD marginal rendering). The mountaineer must *conquer,* knowing that to overcome is to sit with Christ on His Throne (Revelation 3:21). That is the summit!

The call to climb "the steep ascent [to] heaven through peril, toil and pain" is a timely challenge in these days of moral compromise, personal complacency, and spiritual confusion. In the light of this, no one can read *Victorious Christian Faith* and be the same again. Its approach to well-known truths is fresh and refreshing. Some things Alan Redpath says will confirm our faith; other things he writes will change our thinking—and hopefully our living. So once again I commend the book and urge you to read it. As far as I am concerned, it has inspired me to pen these lines:

> I'm heading for the summit,
> I've heard the call to climb—
> To heights that have no limit
> In heav'nly realms sublime.
>
> I'm heading for the summit,
> I see the prize held high;
> I'm pressing on to win it,
> Whether I live, or die.
>
> I'm heading for the summit,
> To see my Savior's face;
> And in the Holy Spirit—
> Exclaim: "I'm saved by grace!"

May you be equally stirred to pray these words and to be challenged anew to head for the summit. Happy climbing!

STEPHEN F. OLFORD

Preface

This book has been written under considerable pressure—pressure on the one hand from a number of friends who have been prodding me for some time to share with a wider Christian public some of the things that the Lord Jesus has been teaching me personally. I appreciate very much their loving persuasiveness, but that by itself would not have constrained me to take action.

Pressures of another kind have been bearing in upon me for some time. One of these is a sense of urgency. I am living on "injury time." If you follow sports, you will recall that in many games the referee will add at full-time so many minutes that have been lost through injury to players. A goal at football, for example, scored in injury time, can turn defeat into victory. Injury time is critical. It is also urgent, for there is not a moment to spare.

I am conscious of being in such a period. I feel an increasing burden, I believe from heaven, like an echo of Romans 8:26 (NIV), ". . . the Spirit helps us in our weakness. . . . the Spirit himself intercedes for us with groans that words cannot express." That which is unutterable becomes utterable as the Lord expresses that burden through us.

Yes, I am heading for the summit of life—a pinnacle both subjective and objective. You remember Paul's great burden for the church at Ephesus when he says:

> . . . I kneel before the Father. . . . I pray that out of his glorious riches he may strengthen you with power through his Spirit in your inner being . . . that you, . . . may have power, . . . to grasp how wide and long and high and deep is the love of Christ, and to know this love that surpasses

11

knowledge—that you may be filled to the measure of all the fullness of God.

Ephesians 3:14, 16–19 NIV

What a possibility, to be filled with all the fullness of God! That is the subjective side of it. But there is also an objective side to life, where we must ". . . press on toward the goal to win the prize for which God has called me heavenward in Christ Jesus" (Philippians 3:14 NIV).

It is with these burdens that I feel bound to put pen to paper—not to glorify myself, for the only good thing about me is the Lord Jesus. Rather do I desire, in the closing years of my life, to plead with all who love His name that together we may by His grace attain the goal and reach the summit where we shall see our beloved Lord face to face.

Also, my dear reader, this book is placed in your hands by the Holy Spirit through me. I trust as you read it you may experience what I have received in preaching it, the blessing of God in a biblical relationship between the Word of God and the experience of God, through the Holy Spirit magnifying Christ in my life. Remember that spiritual growth is not automatic. All the resources of a living Lord are at our disposal, but His requirements of faith and obedience are vital for every day of life until the end of our journey at the summit.

While this book has one continuous thrust, yet each chapter stands on its own to highlight a particular biblical aspect of how to arrive at the summit. It is hoped, therefore, that these chapters may prove helpful to Bible-study groups as well as for individual study.

It is a special joy to me that Dr. Stephen Olford has written the Introduction to this book. In itself it is a masterpiece and comes from the pen of one whose friendship and love in Christ have meant more than I can possibly say over so many years. I know he shares the burden that is on my heart, which is the subject of this book, because he is contantly expressing it far more ably than I can in his own ministry.

Once again, I am most grateful to my dear wife for her typing on the manuscript and for the experience and expertise of Arline Harris in the final preparation of the book.

ALAN REDPATH

Prologue

Hitherto . . . and Henceforth

In this testimony to the Lord's healing, I must begin by relating the experience through which I passed some years ago, a crisis that marked a turning point in my life and led to a dramatic change of ministry. Just two years before, I had returned to Britain to take up the pastorate of Charlotte Chapel, Edinburgh, following almost a decade at Moody Memorial Church in Chicago.

Saturday, September 4, 1964, was one of the rare occasions when we were all together as a family. Our daughter Meryl, her husband, and her two children were with us while she completed her midwifery training in Edinburgh. Then they would leave for the Central African Republic and their first term of service with the Africa Inland Mission.

My wife, our younger daughter, Caroline, and I had just returned from a conference at Hildenborough Hall. We had lunch and a time of family prayer. I was due to conduct a wedding later that afternoon, so I went to my study for final preparation for it and for the services next day.

Suddenly, as I was writing, I lost control of my hand. As I rose to call for help, my legs crumpled under me; my right side was paralyzed and my speech gone. The doctor came immediately and confirmed that I had suffered a cerebral hemorrhage—a stroke. I was in no pain, and my mind was clear, but I was completely helpless. Within a few days my speech returned, at least in part, and a few weeks later I was able to walk a little.

Very shortly, I was scheduled to leave for Southeast Asia. Therefore my doctor felt it advisable to call in a neurosurgeon, who would not allow me to travel until the extent of damage had been ascertained. Into the hospital I went for tests. During one of these, a nerve at the base of the skull was trapped; I lost the use of all the muscles down my left side and suffered considerable pain for several weeks.

The specialist, however, told me I was a "lucky man," because the brain damage was not critical; the fractured artery had occurred at a spot that did not prove fatal. He advised me to forget about further work and to take life easy; then I might live to be ninety years old. If, however, I insisted on getting back into harness, he would not give me more than five or ten years. In the goodness of God, my heart was unaffected, so medically I knew the worst and began the slow process of convalescence.

In an illness of this kind, one's inner defenses are knocked down, and one is reduced almost to childhood. Physically, I could walk only with difficulty; mentally, I felt it was impossible to concentrate or even to think clearly; spiritually, I found that I could not pray or read my Bible. It seemed to me a dark and grim experience, indeed.

Then I became aware of the prayers of God's people around the world. My wife and I were humbled and comforted to receive letters, telegrams, and phone calls from many countries, some of them from people we did not even know. The thoughtfulness and loving prayers of hundreds of fellow believers gave us tremendous encouragement. Our whole family felt the strength of Christian fellowship as never before in our lives.

However, I must confess my reactions to this illness were far from spiritual. So often I had preached that we should never ask, "Why?" in a crisis, but instead, "What lessons can I learn from this experience?" I was now very often asking, "Why?" especially since I had been only two years at Charlotte Chapel, and spiritually we seemed to be on the crest of a wave.

The depths of despair to which I sank were beyond description; sometimes I spent hours each day weeping. I knew God could work a miracle by healing me instantly, should He choose, but did I have the right to expect Him to reverse the laws of nature, which He Himself had created, simply for my benefit? On the other hand, was this illness a chastening from heaven and not an attack from the enemy? Had the Lord made a mistake in permitting this to happen to me? Can there be *any* exception to the truth of Romans 8:28 that "... all things work together for good to them that love God ..."?

Then I found myself being attacked by tremendous temptation. It seemed as if the devil took advantage of my helplessness to throw everything he had at me—sinful thoughts, temptations to impurity, and bad language bubbled up in a shattering eruption. I remember crying out to God at last, "O Lord, deliver me from this attack of the devil! Please take me right Home!"

For the first time in months, it seemed that the Lord drew very near to me. I am sure He was close all the time, even if I did not feel His presence. I had no vision of Him, no dramatic touch of healing. But I do know that a deep conviction came to my heart in which He said, "You have this all wrong. The devil has nothing to do with it. It is I, your Savior, who have brought this experience into your life to show you two things: First, that this is the kind of person—with all your sinful thoughts and temptations—you always will be, but for My grace. I never intended to make you a better man, but to indwell you with My life. Second, I want to replace you with Myself, if you will only allow Me to be God in you. Admit you are a failure and that the only good thing about Alan Redpath is Jesus Christ."

Of course, this was a truth which, in theory, I had known, believed, and preached for many years, but now I know it in my own experience. Romans 7:18 has lived in my life in a new way since that day. "For I know that in me (that is, in my flesh,) dwelleth no good thing: for to will is present with me; but how to perform that which is good I find not."

As I looked back down the corridor of my memory at the past twenty-five years of ministry in London, Chicago, and Edinburgh, it seemed a pattern had been developing in my life, which I had imagined was so spiritual, namely (to quote an old chorus), "To work like any slave for love of God's dear Son." Rarely did I take a day off; little time did I devote to my family—I was always too busy for that.

The Lord showed me that I was putting work before worship. The barrenness of a busy life had taken its toll; my priorities had become twisted. Even my quiet time and my Bible study had become less disciplined than in former years.

Furthermore, I saw that I had become very proud of being orthodox in doctrine, but alas, not nearly so concerned about my obedience to the doctrine I preached. How easy it is to demand a greater measure of obedience from a congregation than one is prepared to give in one's own life! How humiliating to make such a discovery!

This led to a further revelation: I had become much more concerned about the knowledge of truth than about the knowledge of God. Often I turned my Bible study into neat outlines for sermons instead of seeking food for my own soul. Paul's great ambition was, "That I may know *Him,*" not "That I may know *truth.*" To me, the Lord Jesus had become much more a theoretical and doctrinal Figure than a saving, experiential Companion.

As I lay in bed, burdened with such reflections, how ashamed I was that God had given me great privileges and I had neglected them. How I thanked Him for calling me aside to stillness, and how I praised Him, even for the suffering! My heart echoed the words of David, "It is good for me that I have been afflicted . . ." (Psalms 119:71).

The Lord began giving me promises such as Psalms 138:7, 8: "Though I walk in the midst of trouble, thou wilt revive me . . . The Lord will perfect that which concerneth me: thy mercy, O Lord, endureth for ever: forsake not the works of thine own hands." Again, Psalms 118:17, 18: "I shall not die, but live, and declare the works of the Lord. The Lord hath chastened me sore: but he hath not given me over unto death."

A wonderful sense of peace came into my heart. The tensions and strain of the years seemed to roll away from my spirit. I was still very weak, but from that time on I began to experience the divine touch of God's healing hand. Slowly, gently, and very lovingly He restored me to health and strength. There were long months when patience was tested and faith tried to the limit, but I saw with perfect clarity that the Lord's chastening hand had been upon me for a purpose that could only have been revealed to me in the experience through which I had passed.

As I look back, I would not have given up those lessons for anything. Had the Lord healed me dramatically and instantly, what blessing I would have missed! When I cried, He strengthened me with might in my soul and, without reversing the laws He Himself created, He allowed them to work for me in a rich period of spiritual, mental, and physical recovery. For this I praise Him with all my heart.

Sometime later, when I saw the neurosurgeon again, he was amazed. He said that he had never known anybody who had suffered such damage to recover so completely. There was no symptom of my illness left, apart from slight damage to my right hand, which still does not work very well for writing. This is a very minor matter, but a constant reminder of what had been for me a Peniel experience when "... I have seen God face to face, and my life is preserved" (Genesis 32:30).

What the doctor could not be expected to understand, I could see quite clearly: Hundreds of people had been praying for me. Although the Lord had dealt severely with me, the Holy Spirit had spoken to me and shown me the danger of a life lived with wrong priorities. I shall be eternally thankful for the whole experience.

After my stroke, it was perfectly clear that I could not continue in the pastorate of such a large congregation as Charlotte Chapel. My wife and I were faced with a decision: Either I could take a small pastorate, which would be less taxing, or we could believe that God still had a place for me in a wider ministry. We felt it right to choose the front line of the battle. At the end of 1966, reluctantly, yet convinced that it was the will of God, I resigned from Charlotte Chapel.

What should be our next move? We knew only that God had closed one door, but we had not the least idea what lay in front of us. We had nowhere to go, no home to live in, and so we were literally shut up to a miracle. How wonderfully God met us!

First of all, I decided it was right to undertake certain invitations overseas which, in a pastorate, I had previously been obliged to refuse. In the early part of 1967, this took me for five months (on my own) to Africa, visiting areas in Ethiopia, Eritrea, and Somalia, where the Sudan Interior Mission worked, then down to South Africa for their annual Keswick Conventions.

Meanwhile, invitations came for me to return to the United States for varying periods. These I felt it right to accept.

Then our path crossed that of Major Ian Thomas, one of the first of our Christian friends many years ago, the founder and director of Capernwray Missionary Fellowship. "Why not come and live at Capernwray?" he said. "I will build you a house, and you can use it as a base for a worldwide ministry. Then you can lecture at the Bible school when you are home." It did not take us long to make up our minds, and we have been living there since 1969.

What wonderful years they have been! In addition to the privilege of lecturing at the Bible school, to a student body of almost two hundred, composed of students of more than twenty different nationalities, it has been our privilege to go around the world many times. We visited various mission fields, mainly for annual field conferences of such agencies as the Overseas Missionary Fellowship, Wycliffe Bible Translators, Africa Inland Mission, Unevangelized Fields Mission, and others. Also, we have been to various Keswick Conventions in South Africa, Japan, Singapore, Australia, and New Zealand. Included was a three-month tour of five countries in South America.

What can be said of the kaleidoscope of experiences as we look back on them? There have been visits to the Amazon jungles—to Summer Institute of Linguistics base camps in Peru and Ecuador, where around three hundred missionaries assembled for their annual conference. The translators came in from their tribes, and the support teams carried on a minimum of work on base in order to attend the sessions. What wonderful people they were! Each one was a specialist in whatever job he or she was doing, and I felt like a pygmy among giants.

Yet what need! How they came to the conference hungry and thirsty for all God had for them there. They had been drained dry spiritually, as well as mentally and physically in many cases. It is always a privilege to share Christ with such a responsive group, whose dedication to Him is so apparent. If one preaches the Word to missionaries for less than a hour and a half, they complain of being undernourished.

In Africa we shared conferences with the Africa Inland Mission in Kenya, Uganda, Tanzania, and the Central African Republic. In the latter small country, our older daughter and her husband have been working since 1965, and we have had the adventure of visiting them on three occasions. Literally, they are "at the end of the road," being about forty miles west of the South Sudan border, in the midst of the Central African forest. Their isolation is such as few places now experience. In these days of missionary aviation, a plane a month is a luxury for them.

I have found it a joy to speak to believers at numerous conventions that are the outgrowth of the English Keswick. I have seen up to a thousand Japanese Christians, many sitting on the ground, listening in rapt attention first to unintelligible English, then turning with expectant faces to hear the words in their own language from the interpreter. A message takes at least one and a half hours, yet no one moves. These dear Christians, a minority group in their country, eagerly await such conventions, where the Word of God is opened up to them, usually by teachers from abroad.

In these years we have proved that God makes no mistakes. Romans 8:28 is *always* true as one looks back and sees how everything working *together* has shown God's hand and His love at work. The Lord has been teaching me this lesson above all others: Never undertake more Christian work than can be covered in believing prayer. If we are so busy we have scarcely any time to pray, we need to stop and examine our priorities.

The Lord Jesus said, "But seek ye *first* the kingdom of God, and his righteousness; and all these things shall be added unto you" (Matthew 6:33, *italics mine*). At the moment, what is *first* on the list of priorities in your life? If it is anything apart from making Christ preeminent, then you are not heading for the summit.

God has indeed provided for us above all that we could ever ask or think. We miss the close fellowship of a pastorate, but we have gained an ever-expanding circle of friends and a richness of experience we shall never forget. Some of the things we have seen thrill us. Other things frighten us, especially as far as the work of the Lord is concerned.

Several years ago it was said that of one hundred young people offering themselves for Christian service, only one would eventually achieve the goal. It is now said that of young people offering for full-time service (not short-term) and getting out to the field, most of them will last no more than five years.

As I looked around the countries I visited, in many cases I saw the national church growing and expanding beyond anything we know in the West. However, there is a great shortage of trained nationals; they are crying out for teachers and pastors. I find myself asking, "Where is the needed leadership? Where are those who will stand in these places of opportunity?" Many young people are prepared to give the Lord a year or two in a short-term capacity. In some places, this is most valuable, especially where the English language is used. But what happens when the short-term volunteer leaves? A veteran missionary once said, "You cannot hack it with short-termers!"

Where is the necessary dedication, the laying on the altar of all that a person has and is for the service of Christ? This is a great burden on my heart. My prayer is that God will yet use me to challenge young people—and older ones—to a life unreservedly handed over to the Lord Jesus, to do His will: nothing less, nothing more, nothing else.

My life text, which I took from Him soon after my conversion, is Philippians 4:13, J. B. Phillips' rendering being, "I am ready for anything through the strength of the One who lives within me."

Ready for *anything?* I never knew what that would involve, and neither will you. But if you are earnestly seeking the Lord, heading for the summit of life, and asking Him, "What next, Lord?" then you will prove, as I have done, that He is a wonderful Savior, whose grace is always sufficient. As David proclaimed in Psalm 23, God's goodness and mercy follow us every day of our lives, until one day we shall dwell in His house forever.

Victorious Christian Faith

1

The Challenge of the Summit

It has been my great privilege to view, either near or afar, some of the highest mountains in the world. These rocky, snow-capped peaks thrill and awe me with their sparkling majesty, but I do not have the urge to scale them. Some people feel impelled to try for the top. When asked why, true mountaineers answer, "Because it is there!" To them the sight of the summit presents an irresistible challenge.

The apostle Paul truly was a spiritual mountaineer. He issued a challenge to succeeding generations—and therefore to us—to scale the heights of God with him. Listen to what he said in Philippians 3:12–14 (NIV):

> Not that I have already obtained all this, or have already been made perfect, but I press on to take hold of that for which Christ Jesus took hold of me. Brothers, I do not consider myself yet to have taken hold of it. But one thing I do: Forgetting what is behind and straining toward what is ahead, I press on toward the goal to win the prize for which God has called me heavenward in Christ Jesus.

How thrilling his description of the Christian life! How clear and challenging his words! He pictures the believer as one who presses on, full of energy, with a holy discontent in himself, repudiating any thought of having "arrived" in the sense of being conformed to his Lord. Yet he is always climbing, remembering that God's grace is with him and heaven's glory is ahead. This life is only the journey, not his home; life is the climb, not the summit. He keeps his eyes on the crown, his future prize, but today he has a cross to carry—we cannot win the one unless we accept the other.

Let us define the starting point, which we find in verse 12: "Christ Jesus took hold of me." In other words, Paul said he had been "arrested" by Christ. He would never have turned, unless a mighty hand laid hold of him; then all he did was to yield to the pressure and not try to wriggle out of it. The crisis came suddenly; he was checked in full career, as if a mighty voice spoke to a wild and stormy sea and every tossing wave was frozen into stillness.

Few men are saved as dramatically as Paul, but the principle is the same: We are "laid hold of"—gripped and possessed by Christ. Conversion is not a feeble decision one makes; rather, it is God stepping into one's indifference and sinful rebellion, the Holy Spirit invading the citadel of a soul. The initiative is always with God.

Paul was saying, "I press on to grasp and make my own that for which Jesus has laid hold of me and made me His own." Involved in Paul's experience of conversion was the desire to discover the purpose for which God had saved him and to work it out. What was that purpose?

Following Paul's Damascus-road experience, God sent Ananias to tell Paul one thing, ". . . This man is my chosen instrument to carry my name before the Gentiles and their kings and before the people of Israel" (Acts 9:15 NIV). He was chosen for a world purpose, but the effect of his conversion on himself as a man was not mentioned.

Writing to the Philippians, Paul said nothing about that conversation with Ananias. He did not think of himself primarily as called to be an apostle, but summoned to be a Christian. Behind every conversion there is a double objective; we are not saved simply to secure heaven or avoid hell. We are not saved only to be His instruments to bring the Word of God to others. Primarily, like Paul, we are saved, "That I may know him, and the power of his resurrection, and the fellowship of his sufferings, being made conformable unto his death" (Philippians 3:10).

Yes, we are saved to become like Jesus Christ—to live with Him every day, to learn to know Him as a husband learns to know his wife, to be aware of Christ's life formed in us. We are saved to share His reproach in the world, to live by the principle of the cross, dying daily to all but His will and glory; this is the dynamic motive for which God laid hold of us.

We are saved to be a blessing to the world, yes, but the impact of my life upon the world depends entirely upon the impact the Holy Spirit makes on me. In other words, we can have no apostleship without discipleship. Until we learn to live *with* Christ, we cannot effectively live *for* Him.

Whatever we do in life—teach school, care for a home, serve the Lord in a church or on a mission field—these are merely externals. Whether we are active or housebound, called to evangelize a city or the heathen in the jungle, to keep accounts or sweep floors—all that is secondary. Our occupations are just scaffolding around our lives, which sometimes God has to take away until first He has conquered the core of our being, eliciting our love, worship, and conformity to Him.

Is this the summit toward which you are aiming, the outcome you keenly anticipate? It was to Paul, the once-proud Pharisee, who longed to gain the reverence, meekness, and dignity of Christ, which is the peak of Christian experience.

Having made a start, what is our next step? Paul shared with us his great purpose, and as if standing by us and putting his hand on our arm in loving appeal, he said, in effect, "My brothers, whatever some may think of themselves, I know I have not seized the crown yet, but my thoughts and purposes are all concentrated on this one thing.

"As experience after experience comes and goes, falling behind into the past, I stretch out and on to whatever lies before me. Like an eager runner—head thrown forward, body bent toward the finishing tape—I seek for more and still more in the power of our dear Lord as I press toward the goal."

What a picture! What a warning against any thought of "having arrived" spiritually! Judging from the complacent manner of some Christians, one would assume they had nothing left to experience, no more to do or to learn. But there is no spiritual height we may reach here when we no longer have to confess that we are sinners.

The *position* of a Christian is to "be found in Him" (Philippians 3:9)—that is, identified with Christ, which is perfection. One's *condition* is, however, always imperfect yet progressing. His standing in Christ is perfect, but daily he must press on, privileged to be deeply happy and thoroughly humble. A vision of the absolute holiness of his Lord makes it impossible for any Christian to think of himself as being perfected. No, in the power of the Lord he is always seeking a close likeness to Him. That is the purpose we must keep in mind as we climb step by step to higher ground.

Paul saw, further, that the spiritual ascent presented him with a principle to be observed: "I press on," he said. Our conversion is not a stopping place, but a starting point. There will be many dangers and pitfalls, but God always urges us, "Go forward!" Not the pace, but the length of the race often proves too much. Paul looked only to the path before him and the "one thing" toward which he strained with heart pounding and feet racing, because his overmastering passion was to get there as quickly as possible.

No one who continually looks back can win a race. Paul limited himself categorically to "forgetting what lies behind."

Forget past sins, because God forgives them.

Forget past failures, for Satan raises them up to discourage.

Forget past blessings; they may encourage, but they can cause us to live in the past.

Forget past successes, lest we rest on our oars.

After we have learned from our past experiences, we must forget them. Then comes "straining forward to what lies ahead." What a picture! Full stretch, grasping every opportunity to serve the Lord. We must advance in grace so that we may step into every promise of blessing—our daily aim, never to disappoint the Lord.

"Fanatical!" some will cry. Better to be a fanatic and get what you aim for than to be like a sluggish river that spreads itself out over miles of mud, with no current to disperse the stagnation. In the service of evil, their focus on "one thing" spurred on Napoleon, Hitler, Mussolini, and other tyrants who were out to conquer the world. It is the same kind of total focus, centered on the Lord, which inspired William Carey, Adoniram Judson, Hudson Taylor, D. L. Moody, and a host of others to achieve mighty victories in the name of the Lord Jesus.

Paul also saw in life a plan to be obeyed. "I press toward the goal" literally means, "I follow the marked-out course." This includes rules to be obeyed: "An athlete is not crowned unless he competes according to the rules" (2 Timothy 2:5 RSV). Obey the rules and avoid penalties! These rules are found in the Word of God. Therefore admit His Word to your mind, submit to it in your will, commit yourself to acting on it in your life—then present it to others.

Are you on track or off course? Since you left the starting point, have you advanced on the upward climb? Are the same fire and zeal that were given over to self and sin now devoted to Jesus? Or have secondary things crowded out this "one thing"? Concentrate *all* your life on the supreme objective of being made like the Lord Jesus.

However, a journey has to have not only a starting point, but a final goal. Paul calls this ". . . the prize of the high calling of God in Christ Jesus" (3:14). Our goal is not simply the security of salvation or the beauty of heaven, but the ultimate glory of seeing our Lord face to face. One day each of us will be summoned to His judgment seat, where we will receive the prize to which Paul looked forward. "I have fought a good fight, I have finished my course, I have kept the faith," he said. "Henceforth there is laid up for me a crown of righteousness, which the Lord, the righteous judge, shall give me at that day: and not to me only, but unto all them also that love his appearing" (2 Timothy 4:7, 8). We face the climb for our Master's approval, that He may say to us, "Well done!"

If you are weary, if you find the path hard and your feet stumbling, Paul has a word of appeal, "Let those of us who are mature be thus minded . . ." (Philippians 3:15 RSV). The great apostle had already admitted that he was not perfect, but there is a degree of perfection in every stage of physical growth: infancy, childhood, adulthood, old age. There must be no lagging behind at any stage in the Christian life. Are you on schedule? Is your heart set on the slog of the steady climb?

It is sad that some Christians argue, "Why all the hurry? It's all very well to be on the Lord's side, but we mustn't overdo it." They think church is all right, but ask them to come to prayer meeting, to witness or give testimony, and they complain, "That's just too much!"

God will confirm to you the utter worthwhileness of being an all-out Christian. What a tragedy to be among those who profess to know Christ but suffer from arrested growth! Like Paul, may we be found, even in old age, still pressing on.

Paul exhorts us in the next verse, "Only let us hold true to what we have attained" (RSV). You cannot be good at anything without practice, and you cannot remain skillful without continuing that practice. That is true in the spiritual life, also. God's aim is to produce the character of Christ in you. He may choose to do this through sorrow or joy, hope or fear, because for this purpose you were created, redeemed, disciplined, and for this Christ has made you His own.

Maybe your aim is to make a fortune—what then? You want to attain a certain social or business position—what then? You crave to be proved right in all your attitudes and actions or to get stuffed full with knowledge and learning—what then? All these things are worthless compared with the supreme achievement of being made like Christ. God has no favorites, but pours out His Spirit in power to those who obey.

Make Christ your aim: This is the challenge of the summit.

2

Training for the Climb

Every mountain is different. Each has its own distinctive shape, terrain, weather conditions, and hidden dangers. No prospective climber would ever arrive at the base of a mountain that was new ground to him and expect to start climbing. First, he would view the massif from every angle, study the experiences of those who had attempted to conquer it previously, read all he could about it, and if possible, talk with someone who has had close personal dealings with the particular ascent chosen.

Hebrews 12:1, 2 exhorts us, ". . . Let us run with perseverance the race that is set before us, looking to Jesus the pioneer and perfecter of our faith . . ." (RSV).

Here Jesus is called the Pioneer of our faith; He already has tackled the climb and arrived victorious at the summit. It is essential that we study how He was equipped for the task and consider how His victory affects our individual lives.

Look at the opening of Mark's Gospel and notice how Jesus was prepared for His ministry and ultimately for the cross.

Mark's style is blunt, full of rapid movement and action. It is the Gospel of Christ the Servant, but Mark introduced no merely human Jesus. ". . . Jesus [Savior] Christ [Anointed], the Son of God [divine and eternal]" (1:1). The substance of the Gospel is not an ethic, but a Person: the Son who became a Servant in order that He might be our Savior.

Look at the dramatic announcement in verse 9: ". . . In those days . . . Jesus came. . . ." He had been incarnate for thirty years, so this coming was not the commencement of His life, but of His ministry. Jesus set out from the obscure town of Nazareth, from being a workman bearing human responsibilities. There He had grown in

29

wisdom and stature, learning the skillful use of tools. Those thirty years of preparation resulted in a mere three years of ministry.

Three events took place on the eve of Jesus' public ministry, which were essential for all that followed: *Identification*—Jesus came to men and identified Himself with their sin (verse 9); *attestation*—Jesus came to God and was answered with the anointing of the Spirit (verses 10, 11); *confrontation*—Jesus came to the devil and won the duel (verses 12, 13).

These are the principles of God-honoring service in Jesus' Name—for all His people and for always. The absence of these basics makes ineffective the proclamation of the Word of God. For lack of these principles, the church in Western society is in the poor condition that it is.

The key verses of Mark's Gospel tell us how we can apply them to our lives right now: ". . . Whoever would be great among you must be your servant, and whoever would be first among you must be slave of all. For the Son of man also came not to be served but to serve, and to give his life as a ransom for many" (Mark 10:43–45 RSV).

The way Jesus lives among men will necessarily be the way He lives in you and me. He is our life, not just the Patron of our theological system, but our *life;* not just Lord of our devotions, while we continue to live as religious pagans, but our LIFE.

Jesus humbled Himself to take on our human nature. If He had never identified Himself with our sin, we could never be identified with His holiness. Let us consider what these words really mean: "And it came to pass in those days, that Jesus came from Nazareth of Galilee, and was baptized of John in Jordan" (Mark 1:9).

What was John's baptism? ". . . The baptism of repentance for the remission of sins" (1:4). John exercised a ministry that produced repentance in order to prepare for the ministry of Christ, which secured forgiveness. Why then should Jesus be baptized? That is what John himself asked in Matthew 3:14 ". . . I have need to be baptized of thee, and comest thou to me?"

In baptism, Jesus identified Himself with the sins and repentance of the people, not repenting or confessing for Himself: ". . . Suffer it to be so now: for thus it becometh us to fulfil all righteousness" (Matthew 3:15). His water baptism was a preview of His final identification with our sin on Calvary, to save us at the price of His personal crucifixion.

The Servant of Jehovah took upon Himself the burden of human sin as if it were His own. *The Living Bible* gives us a graphic paraphrase of 2 Corinthians 5:21, "For God took the sinless Christ and poured into Him all our sins. Then, in exchange, He poured God's goodness into us!" What amazing identification! Paul reemphasized this in Galatians 2:20, "I am crucified with Christ: nevertheless I live; yet not I, but Christ liveth in me: and the life which I now live in the flesh I live by the faith of the Son of God, who loved me, and gave himself for me."

That means the annihilation of my right to myself. Instead, God's concern for other people is to be expressed in and through me. This is not simply my willingness to die to myself, but an all-out effort to live for Him, to offer my body a living sacrifice so that my every power and gift is brought to the cross to be cleansed and sanctified for His use. People whom God uses are merely ordinary stuff, but they are dominated by devotion to Christ. They become so identified with Him that their lives are spoiled for anything less than His will. We need to be more concerned with our daily dying than with our rights of living.

I shall never forget being at a conference with Dr. Stephen Olford at Columbia Bible College. Following the meeting, two students came up to us and said, "Please tell us the secret of Christian leadership."

Before I had a chance to say a word, Dr. Olford replied, "I will tell you in a sentence: Bent knees, wet eyes, and a broken heart."

What more could be said? Leadership is not the ability to control other people; it is willingness to serve. It is not primarily a theological degree or higher education (though these may have their place). It is essentially the invasion of the Spirit of God to break down my self-determination so that He may endue me with His power. We need to get alone with Jesus and tell Him plainly: Either we do not want sin to die out in us, or at all costs we want to be identified with His death and His saving purposes.

To a very disheartened disciple, Jesus said, "Feed My sheep." That is, "Identify yourself with My interests in others. Let there be something extraordinary and nourishing about your life that can only be explained on the basis of a miracle."

There is a second word in Mark 1:10: *immediately!* Here was heaven's response to Jesus' acceptance of identification. As the NIV puts it, the heavens were "torn open," and the Holy Spirit descended upon Him.

Christ's enduement with the Spirit was accompanied by the attestation of heaven: "And there came a voice from heaven, saying, Thou art my beloved Son, in whom I am well pleased" (Mark 1:11). It indicated God's approval on His blameless life, during the thirty years of obscurity.

This was not the first time—indeed, there never was a time when Jesus was not filled with the Spirit. All He had ever done was done in the power of the Spirit, but on the eve of His public ministry He received a special anointing and enduement of power for service and character, in order that He might experience and exercise the authority of heaven.

Notice that the Holy Spirit came upon Him as a dove, the picture of gentleness. Jesus said His disciples were to be ". . . wise as serpents, and harmless as doves" (Matthew 10:16).

The Holy Spirit descends on us also with all the gentleness of a dove as our submission to and our identification with the Lord Jesus brings attestation from heaven. Then we can say with the Psalmist, ". . . Thy gentleness hath made me great" (Psalms 18:35). We need the Spirit's baptism that we might live, His fullness that we may be like Christ, and His anointing for service. Have we got what we need: the approval of heaven on our lives?

Gentleness was to mark Jesus' ministry and ours. I must stop and ask myself—and you—does that gentleness mark my ministry? Would the Lord ever have spoken to people as I have done? Somehow I doubt it. Have I learned never to deliver a "rocket" without first handing out a bouquet?

The dove was also a picture of lowliness. The poorest of people, who could afford nothing more, were allowed to bring a dove as an offering for sin. That was love reaching down to the lowliest, which Jesus exhibited over and over in His life.

If God is pleased with the gentleness and lowliness of our lives and service, as He was with the life of Christ, what else matters? He looks into our hearts, and when we identify ourselves with His interests and burdens at the price of personal sacrifice, He says, "This is My beloved son, My beloved daughter!" because it is no longer we who live, but Christ who lives in us.

My friend, when that happens, you will not have to be pushed or persuaded into Christian service. You will be aware of an eagerness, a desire that you have never experienced before.

How else do you explain the miracle that took place in the life of that rigid formalist, John Wesley, which turned him into a flaming evangelist? What enabled him to ride 8,000 miles a year on horseback all over Britain, preaching 1,000 sermons a year, mainly in the open air, in all weathers?

On May 24, 1738, in a small chapel in Aldersgate Street, London, Wesley cried out in his heart, "Oh, for the witness of the Spirit within!" Then suddenly he was able to say aloud, "My heart is strangely warmed within me!" John Wesley had been born again in God's Spirit, but from that day on, the fire of the Spirit burned brighter and brighter in his heart.

In a similar manner, his brother Charles was enabled by the same Holy Spirit to write:

> Oh, that in me the sacred fire
> Might now begin to glow,
> Burn up the dross of base desire,
> And make the mountains flow!
>
> Refining fire, go through my heart,
> Illuminate my soul;
> Scatter Thy life through every part,
> And sanctify the whole.

Now we come to a third essential, confrontation. In Mark 1:12, again, we find the word *immediately*. After the testimony, the test. After the dove, the devil. Heaven's approval was followed at once by hell's attack.

Just look at the personnel of this momentous event: the Spirit, who drives—does the Dove drive? Yes! The word in the original is "cast Him out." It is exactly the same word used in verses 34 and 39, dealing with the driving out of demons. So Jesus was thrown into the wilderness—no leisurely walk this, but divine orders into battle. Jesus' resolve was clear in His baptism, and His resources were revealed in His anointing, but then He faced the enemy.

I often wonder, *Did Jesus shrink from it?* The pressure of temptation was intense, and it was sustained for forty days and nights.

Some people can, by a great muster of concentrated effort, resist the enemy, but a prolonged siege to be endured and withstood to the end—that is the supreme test. All temptation is testing, but all testing is not temptation. Jesus had come from Nazareth, where for thirty years He had emptied Himself of all rights concerning His divine sovereignty and had made Himself subject to human conditions.

Remember that Jesus did not need to fight for Himself: He endured this, too, for us. One who has not himself been tempted could never deliver those who are: "For in that he himself hath suffered being tempted, he is able to succour them that are tempted" (Hebrews 2:18).

The first temptation is described in Matthew 4:3, Satan's wily suggestion that Jesus should satisfy bodily craving by using His divine power. "If you are who you claim to be, then prove it," was Satan's challenge. "Turn these stones into bread." It was just as if he had been listening to the voice from heaven saying, "This is my beloved Son." Believe me, Satan is always listening in when God speaks to us, always waiting for his opportunity to counterattack.

What was Jesus' answer? "It is written, Man shall not live by bread alone, but by every word that proceedeth out of the mouth of God" (Matthew 4:4). The Lord was saying, "I am not here to deal with you as God. One day I will do that, but not now. I am here to deal with you as man, on behalf of all other men."

If Jesus had used just one faculty of His divine power for Himself, He could never have been our Savior.

Next, Satan took Jesus to Jerusalem, ". . . and setteth him on a pinnacle of the temple, And saith unto him, If thou be the Son of God, cast thyself down . . ."(4:5, 6). In other words, "Do something sensational to attract the crowd. You have to get people's attention! When the angels come and bear you up, how thrilled they will be! Everybody will flock to you!"

Listen to the Lord Jesus: ". . . Do not put the Lord your God to the test" (Matthew 4:7 NIV). It was as if Jesus replied, "The success of my ministry is not My responsibility, but God's. My responsibility is to obey."

In a last effort, the devil took Jesus up to a high mountain where He could see ". . . all the kingdoms of the world, and the glory of them; And saith unto him, All these things will I give thee, if thou wilt fall down and worship me" (4:8, 9). Nothing could be more opposed to the will of God than for Jesus to worship Satan and accept the kingdoms of the world from him.

What was Christ's answer? "Get out of here, Satan!" For, ". . . It is written, Thou shalt worship the Lord thy God, and him only shalt thou serve" (Matthew 4:10). No wonder we read, "Then the devil leaveth him" (verse 11).

We should not be at all surprised when our attestation by God leads to a confrontation with the devil. Seasons of vision are sure to be followed by trouble of some kind. Blessing is very often followed by battle. After you have received the greatest enlargement of heart, you are most likely to be attacked by the enemy.

Peter wrote, "Beloved, do not be surprised at the fiery ordeal which comes upon you to prove you, as though something strange were happening to you. But rejoice in so far as you share Christ's sufferings, that you may also rejoice and be glad when his glory is revealed" (1 Peter 4:12, 13 RSV). So spoke a much-tempted man.

The wilderness is not the only place of temptation. There is no place where Satan cannot reach us, but there is also no place where the Holy Spirit cannot strengthen us. If He drives us into it, He will be with us through it to triumph. Whether we are defeated or victorious depends upon whose side we take and how determined we are to have victory. By the Holy Spirit, we, too, can answer the devil by the use of the Word of God: "It is written."

After Satan had fired all the ammunition he had, Jesus was unscathed. He said, in effect, "As prince of this world, you can keep the kingdoms. One day they will become the kingdom of My God. I am not interested in returning to heaven by Myself and leaving it an empty warehouse. Rather, I am committed to the redemption of mankind to dwell in the kingdom with Me."

Jesus' goal was the will of God—nothing less, nothing more, nothing else. Chalk it up on a blackboard, brand it in flaming letters on your heart. What is the key to revival? Obedience! From the most anonymous Christian, in the power of the Lord who has already won the battle for us, revival can start. Jesus has bestowed on us His Holy Spirit, who waits for our surrender to win the victory over Satan in us all.

Only after His victory over Satan in the wilderness did Jesus begin to preach. Most of us have finished long before we face an encounter like that.

But then, He knew His "mountain" well. Have you studied your particular mountain? Do you realize that the climb promises to be a stiff one? The summit scaled by our Pioneer, the Lord Jesus, was one that never had been seen before, nor will be again. By reaching the top victoriously, He is abundantly able to give us all the resources we need for our attempt to reach our individual summit.

The outcome depends on you and me; it is governed by our response to the means by which He prepares us for the test. The measure in which our self-pity in the midst of trouble is consumed by a passion for the glory of God is the true measure of our spiritual strength.

In His victory, press on!

3

Resources for the Ascent

Some people say the Christian life is very hard. That is not true; the fact is, the Christian life is impossible! The only One who can live it is the Holy Spirit, when He is released in us in answer to our faith and obedience. Our resources are in Him alone. Why, then, should anyone fear the Holy Spirit?

Fear would be a great hindrance to a mountain climber. Planning any climb, a person must look first to himself: Is he temperamentally, physically, and emotionally fit to attempt such a feat? There must be within him that special quality which will help him in times of greatest difficulty, when he comes almost to the end of his strength and yet he has to push on and up. Unless a climber has the will to achieve, he will fail, and failure on the mountain could mean death. Some men seem to possess great natural resources of endurance and "second wind," upon which they can draw in times of extreme emergency.

The Christian, however, has an eternal supply of heavenly power springing up within him, the power and life of Jesus Christ, imparted by the indwelling Holy Spirit. Today the Third Person of the Trinity seems to be forgotten, neglected, or misunderstood. It is a tragic thing that He who was sent to unite the Body of Christ has become the subject of controversy. How very sad that many people are afraid of Him! Nothing is more wonderful than when the Church exhibits to the world real Christian unity by the power of the Spirit.

Today, unfortunately, the Body of Christ is very fragmented, especially around the subject of the Holy Spirit. I am aware that this territory is extremely controversial, but I believe people need to hear what the Bible says about it. Therefore I am dealing with the ministry of the Holy Spirit from different aspects presented in the Word of God.

I see Christian work today that is so planned that there is little need to depend on the Holy Spirit, and Christian living is so organized that there is little time for the Holy Spirit. He is simply crowded out. Yet the Lord Jesus said in John 15:5 that ". . . without me ye can do nothing." He did not say, "without My help or reinforcement," or, "without an occasional shot in the arm at a Christian convention," but "without My life in you, you can do nothing."

Dr. A. W. Tozer said, "If the Holy Spirit were withdrawn from our churches today, 95% of what we do would go on, and no one would know the difference. If the Holy Spirit were withdrawn from the New Testament Church, 95% of what they did would stop, and everybody would know the difference." That is a strong indictment, but it is true, because today we have substituted committees for Holy Spirit strategy and put program before power.

There is a complete dichotomy in the average (and I am careful to say *average*) church business meeting between the nice evangelical prayer with which proceedings are commenced, the pious benediction with which they are closed, and what goes on between. As men discuss their plans and then ask God to bless them, it is often obvious that the Holy Spirit has not even had a vote.

The Holy Spirit is not an optional extra as if, buying a new automobile, you might order power seats and power windows. The Spirit does not come to produce one superdeluxe Christian in a generation. He does not come to make some Christians first-class and others inferior. He comes to enable each Christian to live what Watchman Nee calls a normal Christian life.

The Holy Spirit is the divine substitute on earth today for the bodily presence of the Lord Jesus Christ two thousand years ago. When our Lord was on earth, the Father said of Him, "This is My beloved Son, hear *Him.*" What God says *now,* we read in Revelation 2:7 (rsv, *italics mine*): "He who has an ear, let him hear what the *Spirit* says to the churches."

First, the Bible tells us plainly that the Holy Spirit has something to say to every Christian and to every church, for the phrase in Revelation is repeated in each one of the seven letters to the churches. Therefore, I must give the Spirit time and room in my fellowship and in my life. Make room for the Spirit to speak, for your Christian life is nothing less than His power let loose in and through you. For that to happen, you must give the Lord time to speak and show you His purpose.

In the second place, it is sufficient that one person hears, initially: "he who has an ear." One person, giving God room and listening to the Holy Spirit, can kindle a spark in a church. One Christian, giving God time, can bring renewal and awakening to his home, his church, and his neighborhood.

Further, this person must have the capacity to hear what the Holy Spirit is saying: The wording of this text implies "he who has an ear *to hear.*" All fruitful service for the Lord begins and continues with hearing accurately what the Spirit is saying. Now, hearing the voice of God has very little to do with the outward ear. The Lord has many ways of getting His message through to those who are willing to listen. He speaks, of course, through His Word, yet the Word without the Spirit is dead, and an experience of the Holy Spirit that is not based on the Word is dangerous. But when the Word is linked with the Spirit, that's dynamite!

The Lord also speaks through a message. Perhaps you have been in a service when the Lord seemed to single you out from the congregation; He talked to you in depth. I have known that experience, on occasion, as I listened to other preachers and found myself under fire from heaven—the Lord was speaking to me *personally.*

He speaks to us through outward circumstances. An example of this occurs in Acts 16:6, 7 (RSV). "And they [Paul and Timothy] went through the region of Phrygia and Galatia, having been forbidden by the Holy Spirit to speak the word in Asia. And when they had come opposite Mysia, they attempted to go into Bithynia, but the Spirit of Jesus did not allow them."

A free paraphrase might well be rendered: "They tried again and again to go into Bithynia, but the Holy Spirit put His foot down and said No."

Acts 16:8 (RSV) says, "So, passing by Mysia, they went down to Troas." *Passing by* means, literally, "plodding through"—just keeping on going on! The open door into Europe came through the slamming of doors to everywhere else.

People come to me sometimes and say, "You know, it is marvelous how every door opened wide! How wonderfully God led me!" I am rather suspicious about statements like that. An open door is not the only criterion of God's will. The devil is very good at opening doors, too. I find that guidance can come when every door seems shut tight in my face and I just don't know which way to turn, but I keep plodding on. Then, when God sees determination to know His will, He will open the right door.

How many of us resist the Spirit's leading in the matter of guidance! We dive into every seemingly open door, get ourselves confused, and make a thorough mess of things. But thank God, He holds the reins in His hand, waiting for the time when we cry out to Him in desperation. In His mercy, and in response to our repentance, God gets us out of the emergency, only to repeat His original instructions, as He did with the prophet Jonah. When a Christian disobeys God, he finds heaven closed to him. The Lord seems far away, and things will continue like that *until* he goes back to the point of disobedience, seeking the Lord's forgiveness.

The Lord also speaks to us through difficulties. Perhaps you have been through some shattering experience, and unknowingly you have turned out of the purpose of God. As a result, He has been giving you a very uncomfortable time. But all through this testing experience He has been holding the reins in His hand, waiting to speak to you about His will for you.

Returning to Revelation 2:7, we can see that all these means of speaking to us are useless unless we have an *ear* to hear, a willingness to "be still, and know that I am God . . ." (Psalms 46:10). Being still is perhaps the most difficult thing for God's people today—to be silent in the depths of their hearts, to shut their ears to their own prejudices and preconceived ideas. Only then are they able to meditate on the principles God brings to their notice and relate them to daily life.

In other words, each one of us must learn to be silent to our own plans and to all our preconceived ideas about how the Holy Spirit should work. Too often we refuse to believe that the Lord can work in any way that is different from the way He has always worked. Only prayer and meditation lead to Holy Spirit enlightenment, for that is God's way of revealing His will to a surrendered life.

That is how the Spirit speaks to an individual and also to the church. Is it necessary to point out that when the Holy Spirit speaks to His people, He does not do it that they may criticize others, but that they may adjust their own lives to the will of God. However, if the Spirit is speaking in relation to a matter of fellowship, then what God has said can be shared with that fellowship to which the believer belongs. No one lives to himself. Everything each Christian does, in one way or another affects the Body of Christ for good or ill.

First Chronicles 12:38 describes an interesting incident. A great crowd came together to make David king. The record says they had learned to "keep rank" (KJV), were "arrayed in battle order" (RSV).

When the Holy Spirit speaks to one of His people concerning something in the church, some matter that needs His attention and about which action must be taken, then the Christian has to learn that he cannot act on his own. He needs to check his guidance with others in the fellowship. He may be right and all the others wrong, but it would be very presumptuous to assume that until all have shared the matter together before the Lord in prayer. It may be some new vision or some line of action that he urgently wants to see carried out. He cannot do it on his own, so he must learn the discipline of fellowship, which will lead to the important adventure of learning to disagree agreeably.

Why is it that so many Christians disagree disagreeably and break fellowship? Paul wrote a letter to the church at Philippi with no criticism in it except concerning two ladies (who might equally well have been men) who were at odds with each other. Paul pleaded with the whole church to gather around and protect them and seek to restore their loving relationship.

It would be a wonderful thing if we all realized that church fellowship is not simply being loving and kind and gracious, but it involves discipline. Therefore, on matters of personal opinion, each must be prepared to sink his opinion to maintain fellowship.

The spiritually alive and influential church is the one where a number of people are controlled by Holy Spirit love and discipline and learn to put aside matters of personal opinion for the good of all. What a wonderful thing it is when Christians, though they begin to disagree, yet continue to love each other! What the churches of our world desperately need is a new baptism of love, a new discipline of fellowship.

Whatever God reveals must be applied first to our own lives, because God does not give us ears to hear in order to criticize other people. Primarily, our lives must be adjusted to His will so that we may learn to love and to work in cooperation with others.

Knowing the fullness of the Spirit is both practical and of utmost necessity. Why be afraid of Him? He never makes demands upon us which, given scope and the assurance of our cooperation and obedience, He Himself cannot meet through us.

4

The Indispensable Counselor

To come to the heart of this subject of the Holy Spirit, I'd like to put a question to you: What do you think a Christian desires most in his spiritual life?

I believe the answer is threefold: first, the assurance of salvation; second, an understanding of the Word of God; third, the ability to make Jesus known to others. If these are not the three main concerns of us all, they ought to be.

This is precisely what the Lord Jesus said when He introduced His teaching on the Holy Spirit for the first time. So that there may be no possible confusion or misunderstanding, we will study in detail exactly what He promised.

John 14:15–17 (RSV) contains the first word of our Lord concerning the essential ministry of the Holy Spirit:

> If you love me, you will keep my commandments. And I will pray the Father, and he will give you another Counselor, to be with you for ever, even the Spirit of truth, whom the world cannot receive, because it neither sees him nor knows him; you know him, for he dwells with you, and will be in you.

The Revised Standard Version uses the word *counselor* where the King James Version uses the word *comforter.* In the last three centuries many words have taken on different meanings. The word here, *comforter,* which has a nice sound, gives us a poor description of who the Holy Spirit is and what He does.

Recently, I read that in the Tower of London there is a tapestry depicting the Anglo-French wars of nearly a thousand years ago.

One section shows the French troops advancing against the English. William of Normandy (known afterwards as "William the Conqueror") is behind them with a long spear in his hand, prodding them into action. The caption over this tapestry is "King William comforteth his soldiers." Some comfort!

Actually, the original meaning of the word contained the implication of "with strength" and, of course, the Holy Spirit is our strength. He is also a Comforter in the sense in which we now understand the word, but there are times when He is the most uncomfortable Comforter I know! If I refuse to accept His will, He prods and pushes. He keeps reminding me about it. If I turn away from His guidance, life becomes very uncomfortable.

I think *Counselor* is the better word, because the Holy Spirit lives within us and encourages us when we seek to do God's will, restraining us when we err from His path, and revealing to our inner beings the mind of the living Lord.

The Holy Spirit is absolutely essential for salvation. The Christian life begins with a miracle, ". . . Ye must be born again" (John 3:7), and God intends that it should continue to be a miracle. When you are born again, the Holy Spirit invades your life; He crosses the threshold and indwells you. Otherwise, you could not be a Christian: "But ye are not in the flesh, but in the Spirit, if so be that the Spirit of God dwell in you. Now if any man have not the Spirit of Christ, he is none of his" (Romans 8:9).

However, you can be a "believer" without having the Holy Spirit. Does that shock you? There are people who have everything correct in their heads; they believe the Bible and are orthodox in their thinking, but they have nothing in their hearts. They become hard, censorious, unloving, lacking understanding in the most important areas of life, even while they boast of their knowledge of theology. How true it is that the letter kills, while the Spirit gives life! (*see* 2 Corinthians 3:6).

Yes, it is possible to be a "believer" without being indwelt by the Holy Spirit. But a *Christian* has experienced the Spirit's invasion of his life at the moment of new birth, to take up residence, never to leave until he arrives in heaven and sees the Lord Jesus face to face. The Spirit has established a relationship that can never be broken—from which you will gather that I believe in the eternal security of a child of God.

In my definition of a *Christian,* which I believe is biblical, I distinguish between a "believer," as such, and a Christian. We are not saved by *what we believe,* but by the One in whom we believe and to whom our lives are yielded. Once that life is given over to the Lord Jesus—and there must be repentance behind that faith—from then on, we live in a special relationship with Him which will never be broken. Of course, if we indulge in deliberate disobedience, we lose our fellowship with the Lord—but not our relationship.

This truth is often illustrated in the home. Any child is apt to be deliberately disobedient and has to be punished. Then for a time the relationship of love seems to be broken. But how eagerly the parents wait for a sign of repentance and sorrow, so that they can go to the child with outstretched arms. The whole family recovers the sense of "belonging" that had been broken by the child's willfulness. At that moment, the child is more precious than ever! One learns the truth that a relationship can never be broken, though a friendship can be severed or an acquaintanceship broken off. But a child is always one of the family. Even though that child were to end up as a criminal or a complete dropout, yet that relationship can never be ended.

Never think that the Holy Spirit has come to patch you up. He knows we are failures with no hope of bettering ourselves. The miracle of the new birth is described graphically by Paul in 2 Corinthians 5:21, "For he hath made him to be sin for us, who knew no sin; that we might be made the righteousness of God in him." What an exchange!

The only good thing about any of us is Jesus. The Lord is constantly saying in our hearts through the Spirit, "Please get out of the way and let Me take control." Then, like Paul, we can say, "I am crucified with Christ: nevertheless I live; yet not I, but Christ liveth in me . . ." (Galatians 2:20). That is the miracle, for the Holy Spirit is essential to salvation.

The Holy Spirit is also essential in order that we may understand the Word of God: ". . . the Counselor, the Holy Spirit, whom the Father will send in my name, he will teach you all things, and bring to your remembrance all that I have said to you" (John 14:26 RSV). Also, "When the Spirit of truth comes, he will guide you into all the truth; for he will not speak on his own authority, but whatever he hears he will speak, and he will declare to you the things that are to come" (John 16:13 RSV). He is essential to the understanding of Scripture.

In talking to a young convert who may be only a few days old as a child of God, I have noticed how the Scriptures seem to light up and come alive for him. I recall when, as a young fellow of barely twenty, in a tavern in the north of England, a colleague from my office pointed me to Jesus, and I received Him as my Lord and Savior. The following Saturday I said to my parents, "I'm not going to play Rugby football today, because I want to read my Bible." They stared in amazement and some concern!

I remember well that sunny day as I sat with my back to the stone wall out in the country and read my Bible—and it lived! I had never read it before. The verse given to me by the man who led me to Christ was Romans 8:1, "There is therefore now no condemnation to them which are in Christ Jesus. . . ," and I underlined that little word *now* so heavily that I went right through to the Epistle to the Philippians and wrecked my Bible. I was very excited because the book lived to me!

There is a grave danger these days for young people—and even older ones—to go after more and more education, collecting degrees and accumulating knowledge. There is nothing wrong with gaining an education and developing one's intellect, but for a Christian all these things are useless without the power of the Spirit—even worse than useless, because often they become substitutes for His power.

Listen to the man in the pulpit who is releasing Holy Spirit power in his life, who is just a channel under God's control, through whom the Holy Spirit is revealing the living Lord Jesus with a tremendous sense of authority. Compare that man with a clever intellectual who is as dry as dust! It ought to be possible to combine the intellectual and the spiritual—and we can thank the Lord for it in many cases. But apart from the Holy Spirit, there is only clever discourse devoid of God's power, which alone can challenge the hearers and transform lives.

The Holy Spirit also is essential to make Jesus real: "But when the Counselor comes, whom I shall send to you from the Father, even the Spirit of truth, who proceeds from the Father, he will bear witness to me" (John 15:26 RSV). "When the Spirit of truth comes. . . . He will glorify me, for he will take what is mine and declare it to you. All that the Father has is mine; therefore I said that he will take what is mine and declare it to you" (John 16:13–15 RSV).

The Holy Spirit makes much of the Lord Jesus; He exalts Him to His rightful place. Sometimes people glorify and uplift the Spirit Himself, which is unbiblical. His ministry is to glorify the Lord Jesus and make the Savior an indwelling reality to all who trust in Him and love Him. Isn't that just what we need today? Paul said from prison in Rome that, as a result of his imprisonment, ". . . Christ shall be magnified in my body, whether it be by life, or by death" (Philippians 1:20).

How do you magnify something? You can take a microscope, which makes little things big—but Jesus is never little. Or you can take a telescope to make distant and remote things come near. How often in your experience has Jesus been remote? If you take off your evangelical mask and come out into the open, you will probably have to confess that often the Lord Jesus has seemed very far away. The Holy Spirit will act as a telescope, bringing Him near and making Him precious.

Finally, the Holy Spirit is essential in evangelism:

> Nevertheless I tell you the truth; It is expedient for you that I go away: for if I go not away, the Comforter will not come unto you; but if I depart, I will send him unto you. And when he is come, he will reprove the world of sin, and of righteousness, and of judgment: Of sin, because they believe not on me; Of righteousness, because I go to my Father, and ye see me no more; Of judgment, because the prince of this world is judged.
>
> John 16:7–11

The Holy Spirit is essential in evangelism because He convicts of sin. But what sort of sin? "Because they do not believe in Me." The conscience warns a person that it is wrong to tell a lie, but only the Holy Spirit can convict him that it is sin not to believe in Jesus. You cannot win people to Christ simply by giving them a tract or a formula of salvation—that may be good, but you do not win them that way. It is the Holy Spirit who convicts someone of sin because he does not believe on the Lord Jesus Christ. That is the Holy Spirit's great work; without His power, evangelism is fruitless.

It is the Holy Spirit who convinces men of righteousness, because

Jesus has gone to the Father. Sin having been dealt with in righteousness at the cross, Jesus Christ is alive, risen from the dead, and He alone can redeem us from its power and penalty.

The Holy Spirit reminds us of judgment—not judgment to come, but judgment past, because the evil ruler of this world already has been judged at Calvary and is a defeated foe. The child of God needs to remember every day he lives that the enemy, though powerful, is helpless before the mighty Spirit of God within. Therefore, the Christian learns not to wrestle with his problems, but to nestle into the heart of the Lord Jesus and leave Him to handle them.

That is where the difficulty comes in; most of us spend a lot of time trying to cope with our weaknesses, concentrating on them rather than on Christ Himself. Never forget that Jesus is exactly the opposite of everything we are. Instead of attempting to narrow the gap between our sinfulness and His holiness—an impossible task— we should be claiming Him in the context of our daily life situations. For instance, if you are just about at boiling point over some issue, turn to the Lord and say, "Lord Jesus, I claim Your grace and patience now. Thank You!" For you can experience only as much of His power as by faith you claim.

5

The Sovereignty of the Spirit

Basically, the Christian life is the replacement of one life by another, an exchange of sovereignties: Self is dethroned, Jesus is enthroned. Nobody can pray, "Thy kingdom come," until first he prays, "My kingdom go." This is Christian revolution!

As we all know, our world seethes with desperate revolution and anarchy; in an attempt to be free, repressed peoples often sink into deeper slavery. Why? Because communist revolution can never change men's hearts. It works only from the circumference and never reaches the center.

The Christian is the greatest revolutionary of all. His revolt has begun at the center. A new Person is in charge, a new King is in control, and the consequences of that should be felt worldwide. Never has the church had such an opportunity to declare this supreme message as it has today, but it seems to be afraid to speak up.

A Christian's supreme task is to display to the world the real freedom that everyone is seeking. The cry of people everywhere is for deliverance from some bondage, but they cannot find it in worldly ideologies, for real freedom is found only in slavery to Jesus. He is not first Savior, and then when it is convenient, He becomes Lord. He is first of all Lord, or He can never be Savior. In the New Testament, Jesus Christ is always referred to as "our Lord and Savior"—the words are rarely reversed. There has to be an exchange of sovereignties, for we are truly free only when we are not free to be free of God.

The Holy Spirit has come to live within the believer for the purpose of administering Christ's kingdom. To apply the kingship of the Lord Jesus is to set a man at liberty: "For the law of the Spirit of life in Christ Jesus hath made me free from the law of sin and death" (Romans 8:2). The downward pull of degeneration is replaced by the upward pull of regeneration by the Holy Spirit, so that the Christian is mastered by a new law, the law of the Spirit of life in Christ Jesus.

Now we see two ways in which the Holy Spirit accomplishes this. First, He is sovereign in salvation: "The wind bloweth where it listeth, and thou hearest the sound thereof, but canst not tell whence it cometh, and whither it goeth: so is every one that is born of the Spirit" (John 3:8). Therefore the Christian life does not depend upon your initiative, but on His.

"Decision for Christ" is a very popular phrase, and because I know what it means, I go along with it. Strictly speaking, however, it is not biblical. Salvation does not depend upon a person's decision for Christ. He said, "Ye have not chosen me, but I have chosen you, and ordained you, that ye should go and bring forth fruit, and that your fruit should remain . . ." (John 15:16). I am so glad that my salvation does not rest upon any initiative I took, but on the initiative the Lord took.

In the 1960s the voices of men speaking came to us from outer space. The Apollo 8 astronauts went farther away from Earth than man had ever been before, orbiting the moon. We listened enthralled on a Christmas Eve as one of them read, "In the beginning God created the heavens and the earth. The earth was without form and void, and darkness was upon the face of the deep; and the Spirit of God was moving over the face of the waters. And God said, 'Let there be light . . .' " (Genesis 1:1–3 RSV). How wonderful to have a Christian with his Bible in a spaceship, talking to men on Earth, hundreds of thousands of miles away!

It is significant that the crew read from the first chapter of Genesis, "In the beginning God created. . . ." God took the initiative. He also took the initiative in our redemption, as we hear the wonderful echo in 2 Corinthians 4:6 (RSV), "For it is the God who said, 'Let light shine out of darkness,' who has shone in our hearts to give the light of the knowlege of the glory of God in the face of Christ."

Charles Haddon Spurgeon, that great English preacher of some two generations ago said, "When you are approaching Heaven, you read outside the gates, 'Whosoever will may come.' But when you are inside and turn around, you see written above the gate, 'Chosen in Him from the foundation of the world.' "

It is impossible to reconcile divine sovereignty with human responsibility—and no one ever has. But if God were small enough to be understood, He would not be big enough to be worshiped. I thank Him for the day when, by His Spirit's sovereignty, I yielded my heart to Him. Then I discovered that I had already been chosen in Christ. As the Holy Spirit does His work in convicting men of sin in order to lead them to Christ, so He takes His appointed lead in effecting their salvation.

In the second place, we find that the Spirit is sovereign in *santification.* There are two meanings to this word: In 1 Peter 3:15, "Sanctify the Lord God in your hearts. . . ," the word means "Set Him apart." In the Revised Standard Version it reads "in your hearts reverence Christ as Lord. . . ." At the very center of our lives there must be one Lord, Jesus Christ. If I am governed by many masters, then I am in bondage to them all and find myself confused by conflicting claims. That was the downfall of Solomon, who began worshiping the gods of his foreign wives. His life of fellowship with God decayed, and his spiritual experience became a thing of the past (*read* 1 Kings 11:1–8).

To be in bondage to Jesus is to be released from every other tyranny. Let Him chain you to Himself, and you will be utterly free. Have you had a coronation day in your life when you stepped off the throne, knelt at His feet, and said, "Lord Jesus, take Your rightful place as Lord and Sovereign of my heart"?

Then we read in 1 Thessalonians 5:23 (RSV), "May the God of peace himself sanctify you wholly. . . ." In that sense, the word *sanctify* literally means, "be made holy." Jesus alone can do that, but He cannot do it alone. Paul warned, in 1 Thessalonians 5:19 (RSV), "Do not quench the Spirit"—do not smother Him, give Him a chance to guide and direct in your life and lead you into His fullness. Many Christians never grow up because they refuse to kneel down.

We must learn to submit; many of us never overcome because we refuse to obey. As a result, there are many of God's children who are dwarfed in their experience, who go to extreme lengths in their search for release from their bondage, simply because they have never learned to submit and to obey. That is where Romans 8 comes in, that great chapter on Christian liberty, the charter of freedom for every child of God. The secret of holy living is there, so let us study it more fully.

First of all, notice that the Holy Spirit conveys a new nature to the child of God: ". . . that by these ye might be partakers of the divine nature . . ." (2 Peter 1:4); ". . . Christ in you, the hope of glory" (Colossians 1:27). Now that new nature is not the old nature regenerated. We receive this new nature at the moment of our new birth, and ". . . Any one who does not have the Spirit of Christ does not belong to him" (Romans 8:9 RSV).

When we receive the Holy Spirit, He takes up His permanent abode in us, to be with us forever: "For by one Spirit are we all baptized into one body . . . and have been all made to drink into one Spirit" (1 Corinthians 12:13). Everyone who is born again has the Holy Spirit dwelling in him. Isn't it an awesome thing to be a Christian? Christianity is Christ-in-you-ity!

You and I are nothing, but Christ is everything, and He is in us from the moment of our new birth. He becomes our second nature. He cannot possibly sin, because He is God, and God can never sin. If He is given perfect freedom in our lives, He will produce nothing but good fruit.

The problem is, alongside the new nature, the old nature continues to exist in the regenerated heart. Some people teach that when a man is sanctified and comes into some mystical second blessing, his old nature is rooted out. If that were so, Romans 8 would not be in the Bible. The old nature is not rooted out. The Christian keeps his old nature right to the end of his life—the "flesh," which is what Romans 8 is all about.

Paul also defined the conflict between the flesh and the Spirit that goes on in every life. In Romans 8:1–14, there are twelve references to the Spirit, and thirteen to the flesh. Side by side, every moment of every day, the new nature that cannot sin confronts an old nature that can do nothing but sin. Such is every Christian's battlefield.

In passing, let us clearly understand the word *flesh*. It is not just what I think is bad about me or my physical body of flesh and bone and blood—it is my whole being. It is all that I am by nature apart from Jesus. Romans 7:18 puts it pretty strongly, especially *The Living Bible* paraphrase: "I know I am rotten through and through so far as my old sinful nature is concerned. No matter which way I turn I can't make myself do right. I want to but I can't." That is the flesh in action.

It is essential to recognize that the old nature, the old life, is absolutely rotten. Too many Christians never achieve a life of victory because they have never accepted the verdict that God has written them off completely. The old nature is impossible to deal with, but the new, sinless nature of Christ is in us by the Holy Spirit.

The easiest way to understand the word *flesh* is to cross off the *h* and read it backwards—s-e-l-f. The flesh is "... sold under sin" (Romans 7:14). Its condition is absolutely incurable, and it is unchanged in the Christian. "For the mind that is set on the flesh is hostile to God; it does not submit to God's law, indeed it cannot; and those who are in the flesh cannot please God" (Romans 8:7, 8 RSV).

Unless you are spiritually proud, you will be prepared to accept God's verdict about you. If you are honest with yourself, you will not be surprised to find that every day of your life your *self* offers unyielding opposition to the Spirit. For example, the Spirit tells you to witness to someone about Jesus, and your self says, "This is not the moment to do so; I'll only make a mess of it." So you keep quiet.

You cannot do anything about that inner self-life—you cannot improve it, polish it up, or refine it. The Word of God says there is only one thing to do with it, and that is to put it to death. According to Romans 8:12, 13 (RSV), it is possible for a Christian to live after the flesh: "So then, brethren, we are debtors, not to the flesh, to live according to the flesh—for if you live according to the flesh you will die, but if by the Spirit you put to death the deeds of the body you will live."

What disastrous consequences follow if a Christian lives after the flesh! In fact, those who continually live according to self-will are betraying the fact that maybe they are not Christians at all. Living a completely self-centered life indicates that one's profession of faith may not have been real in the first place. To quote Charles Haddon Spurgeon again, "If the grace which I profess to have received leaves me exactly the same kind of person as I was before receiving it, it is not New Testament salvation. The grace which does not drastically alter my behavior will never alter my destiny."

That is worth thinking about. If a person is truly born again by the Spirit of God, then his life *must* produce fruit that demonstrates His new relationship with Christ. The Lord Jesus said, in Matthew 7:16 (RSV), "You will know them by their fruits"—and this is still the evidence of spiritual reality.

At Pentecost, something happened that demanded explanation: "What does all this mean?" the listeners asked (*see* Acts 2:12). You have only to read that chapter to find the answer. It was not a new program, not a special organization, but lives that exhibited transformation by the indwelling power of the Spirit of God.

The response of many was, "What shall we do?" (Acts 2:37). Peter's explanation was as clear as daylight: In a word, "Repent, change, dare to be different, and you, too, will receive the Spirit of God."

We can never expect people to ask, "What shall we do?" until they have seen evidence of a miracle in someone's Christian life. We can demand a response, but if we have nothing to explain, no change in character to exhibit, then we have nothing to offer.

6

Life in the Spirit

A climber has to adjust himself to the varying heights and their particular demands, such as differences of terrain and atmospheric conditions. The Christian, also, climbs constantly into new areas of learning and appropriation. By sending the Holy Spirit to indwell our hearts, the Lord provided resources that are adequate for living the Christian life and overcoming the power of the flesh.

"For the law of the Spirit of life in Christ Jesus has set me free from the law of sin and death," said Paul in Romans 8:2 (RSV). We need to understand that the foundation of this deliverance was laid at the cross. The Holy Spirit only fulfills in us what Christ has already provided for us.

Of course, we know that at Calvary Christ bore our sins, but what so often we fail to realize is that He did something more specific: He took with Him our old self and crucified it. Look at Romans 8:3, "For what the law could not do, in that it was weak through the flesh, God sending his own Son in the likeness of sinful flesh, and for sin, condemned sin in the flesh."

His death for our sins was effective only because He died to the principle of sin. We do not become sinners because of sins we commit; we commit sins because we are sinners. *Sin* is the root; sins are the fruit.

People do not easily comprehend the fact of original sin. In spite of our history and contemporary experiences, I find that hard to understand. But have you ever met a child who had to be taught to do wrong? How often a young married couple, thrilled at the birth of their first baby, say of the child, "Isn't he an angel?" It is not long before they realize that something other than an angel has arrived!

S-i-n—at the center of that word is the letter *i*. That is the basis of all the problems in the world today. Hundreds of millions of people, all demanding their own way and standing up for their own rights, are bound to have warfare. Self-will is at the root of every unhappy marriage, the cause of breakdown in the most cherished possession we can have, a happy home.

This is what Jesus came to deal with: He accomplished the victory by Himself dying to the whole principle of self-centered living. Just turn to Philippians 2:5–11. See how the One who was in the form of God from the very beginning did not hold on to His right of equality with God, but emptied Himself. Watch Him coming down the ladder that led Him to the cross: He took human form; He humbled Himself and became obedient unto death, even death on a cross. That was stepping down from the greatest throne in the universe to the most shameful death imaginable.

What was He doing? By His obedience and submission He triumphed and condemned sin in the flesh. That is, He judged it, for when Jesus died, He took with Him to the cross a nature that had never sinned.

Oswald Chambers said:

> The death of Jesus Christ is the performance in history of the very mind of God. There is no room for looking on Jesus Christ as a martyr; His death was not something that happened to Him which might have been prevented. His death was the very reason why He came. . . .
>
> The greatest note of triumph that ever sounded in the ears of a startled universe was that sounded on the Cross of Christ—"It is finished!" That is the last word in the redemption of man. Anything that belittles or obliterates the holiness of God by a false view of the love of God is untrue to the revelation of God given by Jesus Christ. . . .
>
> He became a curse for us by the divine decree. Our portion of realizing the terrific meaning of the curse is conviction of sin, the gift of shame and penitence is given us; that is the great mercy of God. Jesus Christ hates the wrong in man, and Calvary is the estimate of His hatred.

As we repent and believe that Christ died in our stead, you and I become shareholders in His death for our sins. But we also become shareholders in His life, a life that died to the whole principle of sin. Therefore, His Father could not allow Him to remain dead.

In Romans 8:4 (RSV) we read that this was "in order that the just requirement of the law might be fulfilled in us, who walk not according to the flesh but according to the Spirit." How very thrilling! A life that had died to sin reigns in heaven, having been crucified and resurrected, and that life is offered to me. But the crucifixion of my self-life, carried out in principle on Calvary, can only be realized in my experience by the constant working of the Holy Spirit in answer to my assent.

When I yield to Christ, my old nature remains unchanged. Sin has the same hold on it. If I were left to myself, sin would still irresistibly attract me. But the power of the Holy Spirit takes possession of me and ensures a continued crucifixion of the old self, delivering me from sin. The working of His power is in proportion to the submission of my will to Him.

Deliverance by the Spirit is a progressive experience. Some people think that the old self ceases to exist, but there is no scriptural authority for this theory. In fact, Romans 8 disputes it. The word for "crucifixion of oneself" means to render something inoperative. We are dead to sin in Christ, though sin is never dead to us. Our life must grow constantly toward the character of Christ in us, and the Holy Spirit must fill us increasingly.

Up to the very end of our human life, there will be victories to win; daily the self-life must be submitted to Holy Spirit control. If we fail to give attention to that principle, we lay ourselves open to a crushing return of the power of the flesh.

What then must we do to attain freedom through the Spirit? First of all, we must surrender our will into His hands. In Romans 6:13 (RSV) Paul says, "Do not yield your members to sin as instruments of wickedness, but yield yourselves to God as men who have been brought from death to life, and your members to God as instruments of righteousness."

As long as we refrain from resisting God's Spirit, He fills us and frees us. But if we cease submitting, He ceases working. That halt in His operation is brought about not only by open rebellion, but also by our desire to fight with our own powers: That is the characteristic mark of the carnal Christian. We all seem to have a built-in "do it yourself" kit!

If we fight for victory, we head for defeat. Discomfort begins when we reckon we *must* win and seek to do so in our own strength. I have written in my Bible, "Lord, save me from the tension of trying to get my own victories."

How many years some Christians spend—and I confess to have been among them—in trying to fight the battle and trying to overcome! God is never in the self-improvement plan, but always in the Christ-replacement plan.

In a court of law, a prisoner stands before the judge. On trial for murder, he has been found guilty, and his death sentence is pronounced by the law. Then what does the judge do? Does he take out a pistol and shoot the prisoner? No, for he, too, would be guilty of murder. The judge hands the prisoner over to an executioner, who is empowered to carry out the sentence.

Every time Satan attacks with some temptation, I am morally responsible to tell the Lord that I cannot handle it. I need to say, "Lord, this is part of the life from which You died to save me. I hand it over to the Holy Spirit to carry out the sentence of death and to produce Your life in me."

Let me repeat: Jesus is exactly the opposite of all that you are. If you are impure, He is pure; if you are unkind, He is gracious; if you are harsh and critical, He is love. Never spend a moment trying to narrow the gap, but claim Him as the opposite of everything you are by nature. I cannot underline too heavily the teaching of the Bible that the only good thing about any of us is Christ. He stands ready to reproduce His life in each one of us. Only when we place ourselves in His hands, that He alone may command us, will God intervene to sanctify and deliver.

There is no such thing as a war of containment or peaceful coexistence between the Christ-life and the self-life. The question is, How badly do you want all He has for you? You may feel you lack strength of will to maintain constant submission to Him. He asks for no more than a will that is truly sincere, regardless of its weakness. To make your will strong is His business, not yours, "For it is God which worketh in you both to will and to do of his good pleasure" (Philippians 2:13).

Therefore the second part in sharing Christ's life is faith: "So you also must consider yourselves dead to sin and alive to God in Christ Jesus" (Romans 6:11 RSV). As by faith you originally received pardon, so by faith you progress in victory. This requires a definite act of commitment, a starting point from which you never turn back.

As a Christian, you have accepted pardon for past sins by faith, but have you ever yielded yourself to His control and received deliverance from recurring sin, by faith?

Are you controlled by the flesh, or by the Holy Spirit? Have you faith in the power of the Spirit to set you free? Are you living not in your own strength and determination, but by letting Jesus loose in your life?

Faith is two empty hands held open to receive all of the Lord Jesus. You stretched out one hand when you became a Christian and maybe said in the words of the old hymn, "Nothing in my hand I bring, simply to Thy cross I cling."

That is one hand, but what about the other? Is the other hand so full, so busy, that it has never really been stretched out in faith? You took one step of faith to receive Christ. Have you really taken that further step of faith and commitment to the Holy Spirit's control for deliverance from sin? "For sin shall not have dominion over you: for ye are not under the law, but under grace" (Romans 6:14).

Remember, too, the wonderful fact of Romans 5:10 (RSV, *italics mine*), "For if while we were enemies we were reconciled to God by the death of his Son, much more, now that we are reconciled, shall we be *saved by his life.*"

7

The Spirit's Guidance in Service

We find in 1 Corinthians 12 Paul's great pronouncement on the gifts of the Spirit. Why this doctrine is often the subject of controversy, I cannot understand. It is like a nettle, which must be grasped firmly. People urgently need to hear what the Bible says concerning the gifts of the Spirit.

In order for us to understand what Paul is really teaching, we need to consider some words that he emphasizes.

Notice the word *all* in 1 Corinthians 12:13 (RSV, *italics mine*): "For by one Spirit we are *all* baptized into one body—Jews or Greeks, slaves or free—and *all* were made to drink of one Spirit."

In 1 Corinthians 12:28–30 (*italics mine*), notice the word *some*.

> And God hath set *some* in the church, first apostles, secondarily prophets, thirdly teachers, after that miracles, then gifts of healings, helps, governments, diversities of tongues. Are all apostles? are all prophets? are all teachers? are all workers of miracles? Have all the gifts of healing? do all speak with tongues? do all interpret?

Back in 1 Corinthians 12:4–7 (RSV, *italics mine*), the word *same* is repeated: "Now there are varieties of gifts, but the *same* Spirit; and there are varieties of service, but the *same* Lord; and there are varieties of working, but it is the *same* God who inspires them all in every one. To each is given the manifestation of the Spirit for the common good."

What does all that teach? Very simply this—that the Lord knows what is best for each one of us, in order that we may fit into His Body, the Church, and take our part in it. None of the gifts men-

61

tioned in this chapter—fourteen of them—are natural talents. Look at the list in verses 8–10: wisdom, knowledge, faith, healing, miracles, prophecy, tongues, and so on. But we can have none of them unless the Holy Spirit is in control.

It follows that nobody should envy someone else's gift, for "All these are inspired by one and the same Spirit, who apportions to each one individually as he wills" (12:11 RSV). All the gifts are needed within the fellowship of the church.

In 1 Corinthians 12:14–21 there are no less than seventeen references comparing the church to the physical body: The foot and the eye, the hand, the head, and so on, all unite to make up the body. We learn that no part of the body can say that other parts are unnecessary. Nor can a member say, "I don't belong."

Paul stresses a further important point, that every member should care for the others: "And whether one member suffer, all the members suffer with it; or if one member be honoured, all the members rejoice with it" (12:26).

His final point is that the unifying life of the Holy Spirit is the answer to all carnality. Verse 25 (RSV) says, "that there may be no discord in the body, but that the members may have the same care for one another."

Have you ever walked along, and a thorn pierced your foot? What happened? You stopped. Your brain had received a message from your foot saying, "I am hurting!" Then your eyes looked down, your hand moved, your back bent, your knees flexed, and you stooped down. Every part of your body attended to removing that thorn from your foot. Every part of the body was concerned about the small member that was in pain. That is how it should be in the Christian church, for Paul says if one member suffers, all suffer with him.

This area of caring for one another is very neglected, because so few of God's people are willing to get involved with those who are in desperate need. It is easy to put money in the offering plate, but often very hard to give the love, time, and care that are involved in meeting people at their place of need.

One of the things we all need is to feel convinced that our place in the Body of Christ is not of our choosing. Neither is it the result of the appointment of others. I am where I am, and what I am, by the sovereignty of the Holy Spirit. Therefore I will not hand in my resignation when the pressure gets hot!

I recall a man saying to me, "I want you to know that I have had seventeen pastorates."

I raised my eyebrows and said, "Really? Pardon my asking, but how old are you?"

"I am just forty-five," he said.

I got the picture—maybe not the one he would have liked. Every time the "honeymoon" was over, he left. Whenever there was criticism or he did not get his own way, he ran away from the situation. He had never realized that his place in the Body of Christ was by divine sovereignty, not by personal choice or by the appointment of others. Only the assurance of God's assignment in a man's heart can enable him to take the pressures.

Because God gave it to him, no child of God should ever feel dissatisfied with the place he has in the Body. He should never be envious of the places of others, because the function God has entrusted to him is uniquely his own. Read again 1 Corinthians 12:11 (RSV): "All these are inspired by one and the same Spirit, who apportions to each one individually as he wills."

Nobody since Pentecost has ever had or ever will have all the gifts of the Spirit. Of course, the list of gifts in this chapter is incomplete. There is a further list in Ephesians 4, which includes evangelists and pastors. Romans 12 lists the gifts of serving, exhorting, and giving. The New Testament mentions some twenty gifts, and no one can have them all.

But it *is* possible to have all the fruit of the Spirit, which is described in Galatians 5:22, 23 (RSV): ". . . love, joy, peace [our relationship to the Lord Jesus], patience, kindness, goodness [our relationship to fellow Christians], faithfulness, gentleness, self-control [our relationship to ourselves]. . . ."

That list describes the character of the Lord Jesus. When we are filled with the Spirit, we are filled with the living Lord Jesus (Ephesians 5:18), who will reproduce all that fruit in us. The Christian must make it his aim daily and increasingly that his life may reveal all the fruit of the Spirit—even though he cannot have all the gifts.

Therefore, nobody has a right to demand that others should have his particular gift. Because a person has a gift, especially a more dramatic one such as tongues, healing, or prophecy, he should not judge others on the basis of whether or not they have that particular gift. But *all* of us should exhibit the fruit of the Spirit. I do not ask for a manifestation of gifts apart from fruit, nor of fruit apart from the gifts. Both of them should be combined in an effective witness for Christ.

The gifts of the Spirit are related to ministry, service, and witness, and the Lord is sovereign in their distribution. The fruit of the Spirit is related to character, and all of us are commanded to be filled up with Jesus, in whom is all the fullness of God (*see* Colossians 2:9, 10).

It should be clear (though apparently it is not always so) that to make speaking in tongues an essential evidence of baptism in the Spirit is quite unbiblical. In the first place, not all Christians can have this gift: "Do *all* speak in tongues? Do *all* interpret?" Obviously, the expected answer is "No."

If speaking in tongues were the most important thing that every Christian should have, it would be prominent in every New Testament church letter. Instead, it is mentioned only in this particular epistle, in only three chapters, and always with a view toward keeping it under control. Furthermore, to speak in tongues gave no evidence of spiritual maturity, for the Corinthian church was utterly carnal, yet they claimed to possess that gift. There is great danger in centering upon an experience. The great need is to center upon the Word of God, and when experience does not agree with the Bible, there is something wrong.

The second reason is that the phrase "baptism in the Spirit" needs to be defined from Scripture: "For by one Spirit we were *all* baptized into one body. . . ." All who have been redeemed by the blood of Jesus have experienced this, for baptism in the Bible always refers to an initiation. It is therefore used to mark the beginning of Christian experience, with all—every believer—being baptized into one body.

". . . *All* were made to drink of one Spirit"—that happened at our new birth. In Acts 1:4, 5 (RSV), the risen Lord said to His disciples, ". . . Wait for the promise of the Father . . . before many days you shall be baptized with the Holy Spirit." That happened on the Day of Pentecost: "They were all filled with the Holy Spirit . . ." (Acts 2:4 RSV).

Baptism and fullness are used synonymously in that case, but in the book of Acts, there are only two other occasions on which we read of the baptism in the Spirit. In Acts 10, there was a "Pentecost" for the Gentiles in the house of Cornelius. In Acts 19, Paul found some Ephesians who had experienced John's baptism, and after he told them about Christ's death and resurrection, they received an overwhelming experience of the Holy Spirit.

Many times after Pentecost we read that the believers were "filled with the Spirit" (*see* Acts 4:31; 7:55; and so on).

On one occasion the word is used in reference to our Lord—in Luke 12:50 (RSV), when He said to His disciples, "I have a baptism to be baptized with; and how I am constrained until it is accomplished!" In that sense He used the word concerning an overwhelming experience, His initiation into death.

Confusion arises when one of these words is stressed at the expense of the other. Baptism into a new relationship with the Lord—when we are born again—occurs once. The filling of the Spirit for the growth of that relationship toward Christian maturity occurs over and over again. There is only one baptism, but there are many fillings.

To some people, and I number myself among them, who for many years may have had a very nominal Christian experience, when their spiritual lives were in total chaos—to such a person can come a confrontation with the Lord Jesus of such impact that his life is turned upside down and inside out. It is an overwhelming experience, and that new commitment is indeed like a fresh baptism. I would not quarrel over terminology, but I know from experience that the moment a man discovers the truth that the Christian life is ". . . not by might, nor by power, but by my spirit, saith the Lord of hosts" (Zechariah 4:6), there is a tremendous release of tension.

Many years ago, at a meeting at which I was present, when I was a young man in a desperate backsliding state, Major Ian Thomas said, "What do you think God expects of you?"

As I thought of the high level of Christian attainment that alone could please God, I curled up inside and felt totally discouraged.

"God expects nothing from you but failure!" Major Thomas continued, "*but,* God has given the Holy Spirit to you that you need not fail!"

Like a flash I saw it. In myself, I was absolutely nothing. That was why the cross was in the Bible: If I could do anything at all to remedy my failure, the cross was simply a long-ago tragedy. But because it was impossible for me to do anything for myself, the cross was necessary and Jesus came to die on it. He came for failures. He came for sinners. He came for people at the end of their rope, who just cannot take any more, who are helpless to lift themselves from the pit of despair.

Into that arena of failure comes the Holy Spirit to live out Christ's life and His power in and through those who will come to Him in their desperation. That discovery, which may take place at their new birth (but which, in the majority, seems not to do so), is like being born again all over again! Therefore I can understand people saying, "I've been baptized in the Spirit."

Personally, I prefer using the biblical words "the fullness of the Spirit." When I was born again, I was baptized by the Spirit into the Body of Christ. Then when I realized what a failure I was, because I had Jesus, but He never really had all of me, when I yielded fully to Him, I experienced an overwhelming sense of His filling and power!

Over the past decade and more, I have traveled all over the world. I have found that the greatest impact for Christ in this century has been through the "charismatic movement," or ministry of renewal. It is far greater than any question of speaking in tongues—the glossolalia. To talk of someone being "charismatic" immediately calls to mind a person who speaks in tongues, but that is not accurate.

What does the word *charismatic* mean? Actually, that everything you and I have received is a gift of the grace of God. If we do not have that, we are not born again. Every Christian, in the biblical sense, is a "charismatic" Christian, having received from the Lord His grace and His gifts. Because of a confusion of terminology and a variety of interpretations of words, tragic division has been caused among God's people.

Whenever there is a valuable reality, there arises also the counterfeit. The insistence of some that everyone should have that one particular gift of tongues has completely disillusioned many Christian people. That view is unscriptural and incorrect, but because of it, many react by saying, "Don't have anything to do with this teaching on the Holy Spirit. We have everything we need in Jesus—we've already got it all!"

Excuse me, but if we have it all, then what is the matter with us? Why are we impotent Christians? Where is that vital New Testament impact? Why is the church today ineffective and the world outside disinterested and untouched? I refuse to be put off by counterfeits and misdirections, because my heart hungers more and more for Jesus and a fresh infilling of His Holy Spirit every day. Romans 12:1 gives a command that should be a daily prayer and commitment: ". . . present your bodies a living sacrifice. . . ."

I am so glad that I held these beliefs about the gifts and working of the Holy Spirit before there was such a thing as the "charismatic movement." Yet I cannot fail to be impressed by the fact that worldwide, many churches have received a fresh touch of Holy Spirit life and power. All that had been substituted for Holy Spirit power has been forgotten, and the Spirit of the Lord is moving. The world outside is seeing a difference and taking notice.

I have seen churches that were absolutely dead come alive—and I noticed that the first thing that strikes one upon entering the building is *love*. There is that warm sense of a caring and sharing people who love the Lord and also love you.

Some people would tell us that certain gifts of the Spirit—prophecy, healing, and tongues in particular—were withdrawn in the first century and are not meant for this age. How can we arbitrarily dispense with these gifts? Maybe we don't understand them, or perhaps we are afraid of them—yet we accept all the others gladly. We cannot do that with the Bible. I believe the church will need to exercise all of the gifts in love, being careful, of course, that they are used under the direction of the Holy Spirit.

In these last days, when Satan is turning on all his power against God's people (as evidenced by the rise of Satan worship, witchcraft, and the occult), a true manifestation of the gifts of the Spirit may be God's method of revealing His power in opposition to that of the forces of darkness. The enemy is cramming on intense pressure, and at the same time the weakening church, by and large, seems afraid of the available power of the Holy Spirit.

One evidence of reality in possessing these gifts, I believe, especially the gift of tongues, is that those who have received that gift never talk about it or seek to propagate it. As 1 Corinthians 14:2 makes perfectly clear, the gift of tongues is for worship, to make the Lord real in one's own personal prayer life—and not primarily for witness.

To sum up, it is not correct to say that certain gifts were dispensed with in the first century. We need all the gifts in the whole church today in order to stand our ground in warfare against the devil. If the Body of Christ is not availing itself of all God's provisions for victory, then it is doomed. What answer has the nominal church and the nominal believer to the pressures of today? Without the special anointing of the Holy Spirit and the gifts He provides, we are all bankrupt.

Concerning the gift of tongues, I know of many dear friends who have been at the end of their rope and in their desperation and failure have cried to the Lord, and He has met them. They have received a fresh fullness of the Spirit and also the gift of tongues. But they would never tell you unless you asked them; all that is seen by others is Jesus shining through.

There are many people who speak in tongues, but who show no evidence of being filled with the Spirit. Likewise, there are many people who are filled with the Spirit but do not speak in tongues. May the Lord help us to keep this whole thing in balance! We need to remember what Jesus Himself said was the function of the Holy Spirit: to make Him real, to make the Bible live, and to enable His people to witness for Him effectively.

So let us get our priorities right. 1 Corinthians 14:12 (RSV) reads, "So with yourselves; since you are eager for manifestations of the Spirit, strive to excel in building up the church"—and not in tearing it apart. Remember that between chapter 12 and chapter 14 in 1 Corinthians, strange to say, comes chapter 13! Because it is there, 14:1 (RSV) reads, "Make love your aim, and earnestly desire the spiritual gifts."

8

The Way to "Up" Is "Down"!

After a mountain-climbing expedition is formed, the task of selecting adequate equipment for scaling the heights raises important questions. How much is rock? How much is covered with ice and snow? Every surface needs varying types of clothing, footwear, and implements. So the climbers sort out their crampons, select their pitons and ropes, decide whether or not they will require oxygen. They check and recheck their gear to be quite sure that nothing essential is left out.

God has given us adequate equipment for whatever task He sets before us. Let us look at this equipment, but also look at our own lives to find out in what areas we may be lacking. The Lord has resources to meet every need, every challenge, every obstacle that confronts us. All He asks is that we recognize our own insufficiency. As we accept the challenge and open our lives to receive all God has for us, He makes it available through the indwelling Christ in the power of the Holy Spirit.

Many Christians are discouraged, defeated, and disillusioned, carrying heavy business responsibilities, the pressure of which proves sometimes too great. Their testimony suffers, and often they snap under the strain. There are men in the ministry who find that the burdens and claims of their church members prove too much, and in spite of their training, they discover they just do not have what is required. There are housewives with the care of teenagers, whose husbands do not seem to understand or take their share. Students are on the verge of giving up because they are so disillusioned. They find themselves stuffed full of knowledge, but spiritually, they are shriveled up.

Do your recognize yourself in any of those categories? If you do, you urgently need to do some heart searching. Why do we believe so much but experience so little? The head is full of learning, but the heart is empty. We get so frustrated that the Christian life seems to us either a myth or unattainable.

To discover some of God's purposes in redeeming us, we will study part of Ezekiel 47. I am not unmindful of the future fulfillment of this prophecy in the millennial age, when the Lord Jesus, in visible glory, will reign in Jerusalem. But in this chapter we also find a graphic illustration of resources for Christian living.

The Bible is an Eastern book, and many of its word pictures reflect that setting. For example, the people of that land knew the value of water. Often the ground was hard as iron; rain was scarce and every drop precious. A river made the difference between a desert and a garden. It is not surprising that many references to water are found in Scripture, such as "wells of salvation," "floods on dry ground," and "streams in the desert."

In the New Testament, the Lord Jesus used the same metaphor in John 7:37, 38 (RSV), ". . . If any one thirst, let him come to me and drink," and, "Out of his heart shall flow rivers of living water." Finally, in Revelation 22:1 are these glorious words, describing the New Jerusalem, where there will be no sun or moon, no sorrow or sin, but ". . . a pure river of water of life, clear as crystal, proceeding out of the throne of God and of the Lamb."

The apostle John explained that Jesus spoke ". . . of the Spirit, which they that believed on him should receive . . ." (7:39). Ezekiel described a great river and recorded that God said everything would live where the river flowed. Put these two thoughts together, and we find that God's promise is linked to our longing, if it is our hearts' desire that the barrenness within us might be transformed into a garden. Like an electric train during a power failure, we have everything except the spark that moves us forward.

Let us look at Ezekiel 47:1 (RSV): "Then he [the angel] brought me back to the door of the temple: and behold, water was issuing from below the threshold of the temple toward the east. . . ." Here was the source of the river's power: It proceeded from the threshold of the temple, from the mercy seat, the very Throne of God. All true blessing that we can ever know originates with God.

What assurance it brings us to know that the flow of God's Spirit has its beginning in the Throne to which the Lord Jesus has been raised. There justice has been satisfied, and there our Lord received from the Father the promise of the Holy Spirit (*see* Acts 2:32, 33). Yet it is a throne, so there should be no careless approach on our part. There should be awe and reverence—what is often called "the fear of the Lord"—as we realize the divine source of the power that indwells us. Every Christian, on receiving the Spirit of God, receives "throne life." You may never yet have tasted the victory, but certainly you have the Victor.

Now look further at the course of the river: "... the waters came down from under from the right side of the house, at the south side of the altar" (47:1). That is, by way of the place of sacrifice. The only way the life-giving stream of Holy Spirit power can reach the world is by way of the cross; until Jesus was glorified, the Holy Spirit was not given. The Spirit comes to my heart because Christ's blood has been shed and sin has been put away. Therefore, His coming to my heart and life is the ordained outcome of Calvary. But we seek for His presence and power in vain until, in true repentance and faith, we meet Him at the cross. Calvary precedes Pentecost—that is as true in experience as it was in history. We long for Pentecost, but often we are unwilling to go by way of Calvary.

Look at the force of the river, which grew in power and depth until, only a mile from its source, it was too deep to ford. No tributary had entered it, nor was it reinforced by any other stream. It owed its growth and power to the constant springing up and pouring forth from its source in the sanctuary.

Whenever God can find a human channel ready to receive Him, He gives the Holy Spirit without measure. We can add nothing to His power: Too often, our plans and programs only choke it. We can no more live the Christian life than we can achieve our own salvation. In the Lord Jesus Christ, God has provided for us all that we need to live triumphantly in any circumstances.

By faith in a crucified Lord, you received forgiveness. At that moment you were sealed and indwelled by the Spirit, who can meet every demand upon you as you assent with faith and obedience to the will of God. You may possess all the academic, intellectual, and even spiritual know-how, but if you have never learned to tap the resources that are yours in Christ, sooner or later your life, hopes, and dreams will lie in shattered ruins. "For," said the Lord Jesus, "without Me you can do nothing."

As we go on, please notice the experience of the river's depth in Ezekiel 47:3–6 (RSV):

Going on eastward with a line in his hand, the man measured a thousand cubits, and then led me through the water; and it was ankle-deep. Again he measured a thousand, and led me through the water; and it was knee-deep. Again he measured a thousand, and led me through the water; and it was up to the loins. Again he measured a thousand, and it was a river that I could not pass through, for the water had risen; it was deep enough to swim in, a river that could not be passed through. And he said to me, "Son of man, have you seen this?"

Have you noticed the threefold repetition of the phrase, "he brought [or led] me through . . ."? How far has He brought you through, and what is your present depth in the outpouring river of God's Holy Spirit?

He "led me through the water," the prophet wrote in verse 3, "and it was ankle-deep." This suggests the spirit of faith that enabled you and me to claim salvation and to receive life—but we are only ankle deep. There is still a large amount of self showing and very little evidence of the flow of Holy Spirit life.

This is the condition of the carnal Christian described by Paul in 1 Corinthians 2:14 and following. He said the people there were living in spiritual infancy; they were selfish and showed little concern for others. They evidenced no growth, no ability to feed on God's Word, and little desire for it. They sustained spiritual life by being spoon-fed with the "milk" of the Word (1 Corinthians 3:2).

Not one of those Corinthian Christians began their walk with the Lord Jesus in that state. They would have been spiritual, longing for more and more of what Paul was telling them about the wonderful Lord and Savior to whom they had just been introduced. But they had sunk into indifference, living on a worldly level, touchy and resentful. When we meet Christians of that kind, we find ourselves far more conscious of them than of the Master. How critical they are of others! How jealous of their own success and how unloving in speech!

Is *that* all our God has provided for His children? Heaven forbid! If we stay only ankle deep in the river of life, we misrepresent to the world the fullness of Christian experience and show our own sinful nature instead of reflecting Christ. Yet it is possible to be in this state and still be indwelled by the Holy Spirit. Such an experience is described in Romans 7: born of the Spirit, yet ruled by the flesh. The ankle-deep, carnal Christian is mastered by the flesh, the world, and his own selfish desires. He flounders on the brink of the river, often totally confused about the real meaning of the new life he is supposed to be enjoying.

Has the Lord brought you through that? I trust that He has.

Let me say a word of caution: The biographical experience of a child of God is not automatically from the natural to the carnal and then to the spiritual. That is, he does not progress from Romans 4 and 5 to chapter 7, and then on to chapter 8. You may leap from chapter 4 to 8, then lapse back to chapter 7.

Look back to the time of your conversion. Surely then you knew peace and joy and relief from your burden of sin. You had repented and been forgiven, and like Christian in *Pilgrim's Progress,* you felt like giving three leaps for joy! You had received "throne life," and the Lord had filled you to capacity. You had all you could take in of Him.

In response to continued faith and obedience, He was waiting to fill you with all of Himself. But did that actually happen? Or did you have the experience—like many Christians, including myself— of failure to go on with God, of being defeated and maybe going through years of backsliding? You had been spiritual, but you lapsed into carnality, and the tide of Holy Spirit life, which had been coming in, was rapidly going out. Such is the "ankle-deep" experience.

"Again he ... led me through the water," Ezekiel said, "and it was knee-deep." The spirit of prayer is suggested, for when the knees are captured for God, there are indications that the tide of blessing is rising. Here is a man hungry for more of the Lord, desperate for a touch of life from heaven, and conscious that he just cannot go on as before. So he is on his knees.

Such a person reminds me of Jacob in Genesis 28; on his first night away from home, scared of his brother, he met God at Bethel. He dreamed of angels ascending and descending on a ladder from heaven to earth, and the Lord spoke to him comfortingly, promising His presence and protection. Jacob made a bargain with God: If God would prosper and protect him and bring him home safely, he would trust Him.

But everything went wrong. Jacob married the wrong girl, became a partner in business with an unbeliever, and for twenty-one years his life was at a stalemate. Then he found himself being deceived as previously he had deceived others.

God spoke to him again and told him to return home. So Jacob packed up his belongings, wives, and family and set off home, only to hear that his brother Esau was approaching. Sending his family on ahead, he stayed by the brook Jabbok (*see* Genesis 32) and "a man wrestled with him until the breaking of the day" (RSV).

It was the Lord, who had met him more than two decades previously, who now said, "Let me go, for the day is breaking."

But Jacob insisted, "I will not let you go, unless you bless me" (RSV), and he clung to Him. That is desperation, knowing that you cannot go on any longer living as you have been, on a shockingly low level of Christian experience. You get on your knees and tell the Lord you won't let go until He blesses you.

Do you recall what the Lord asked Jacob in Genesis 32:27 (RSV): "What is your name? . . ." As if He didn't know! Of course He knew. The Lord was not asking for information, but for confession. Jacob gave Him the answer as if to say, "Sorry, Lord, but in spite of all your goodness and faithfulness to me, I am still Jacob."

The Lord replied, "Your name shall no more be called Jacob, but Israel . . . (RSV)." No more a cheat and deceiver, but "a prince with God." That did not happen in a moment. The transforming process took many years, but from that time on, the "Jacob life" began to die out and the "Israel life" began to emerge.

Tell me, what is *your* name? What do you say to God when He asks that question? Honest confession leads to brokenhearted repentance; that is what has to occur if your name and character are to be changed.

After the Lord "arrested" Paul on the Damascus road, He prepared a very humble follower, Ananias, to shepherd Paul in his new Christian life. But Ananias, having heard about Paul's persecution of Christians, was afraid. The Lord reassured him by adding, ". . . for behold, he is praying" (Acts 9:11 RSV). What was strange in that? Paul the Pharisee had spent half his life saying his prayers! Yes, but now the Lord heard him, for he had repented and was on his knees before God.

It was not a question of, "Behold, he believes this and that," or, "Behold, he gives his testimony, sings, and plays the trumpet," but, "Behold, he prays." This is what the Lord longs to see among His people. If only there were a great soul thirst for God in the church today! We can never expect the world to thirst for God unless first we thirst for Him. Alas, it is too rarely found because Christians are too often content with past experience and do not wish to be disturbed.

In his book, *The Pursuit of God,* Dr. A. W. Tozer wrote these trenchant words:

> Everything is made to center upon the initial act of accepting Christ. We are not expected thereafter to crave any further revelation of God in our souls. We have been snared in the coils of a spurious logic which insists that if we have found Him, we need no more seek Him. This is set before us as the last word in orthodoxy. The heart theology of a grand army of fragrant saints is rejected in favour of a smug interpretation of Scripture that would have sounded strange to Augustine, Rutherford, or Brainerd. O that the language of John Samuel Monsell were in our hearts again!

> I hunger and I thirst;
>   Jesus, my manna be;
> Ye living waters burst
>   Out of the rock for me!

> For still the desert lies
>   My thirsting soul before;
> O living waters, rise
>   Within me evermore.

Christian, get down into the river until your knees are submerged! Has He brought you through?

Now look at Ezekiel 47:4 (RSV) again: "He . . . led me through the water; and it was up to the loins." Here is the picture of power. Deeper in the river, the man has discovered the secret of strength: "They that wait upon the Lord shall renew their strength . . ." (Isaiah 40:31) or, "They shall exchange their strength for His." Paul said, "I can do all things through Christ which strengtheneth me" (Philippians 4:13).

Here is the revolutionary discovery! The Holy Spirit is in me to meet every demand upon me that is within the will of God. Victory comes, not through my struggle, but in His power and through His mighty energy.

This is the secret of the exchanged life: Has He brought you through?

"Again . . . it was a river that I could not pass through . . ." (47:5). The man was swimming in the river, completely out of his depth. When a person is swimming, he is invisible except for his head, and the head of every Christian is Christ. Here indeed is all fullness of blessing, realized only when self is immersed and others see Jesus only.

Just a mile from the source of the river, it was deep enough for the man to swim in! How many miles are you from the source of your Christian life, and how deep in the river of God's blessing are you? All Christians have eternal life, but not all have the abundant life of which the Lord Jesus spoke in John 10:10, "I am come that they might have life . . . abundantly."

As we study this particular passage from God's Word, just where do we fit in? Only ankle deep? Or is the water to our knees, or even to our loins? Or are we swimming in the glorious experience of the fullness of the Holy Spirit, which makes the life of the Lord Jesus real to us in a very personal way?

There is a final thought, recorded in Ezekiel 47:6–12, where we are told the effect of the river's flow. Just considering the essence and energy of the Spirit and looking at the experience of those who open their lives to Him is incomplete without noticing the effect of such action. The way to "up" is "down" right enough, but what is the outcome of such an overwhelming work of the Holy Spirit upon us. Is it worth it?

Now read Ezekiel 47:12 (RSV): "And on the banks, on both sides of the river, there will grow all kinds of trees for food. Their leaves will not wither nor their fruit fail, but they will bear fresh fruit every month, because the water for them flows from the sanctuary. Their fruit will be for food, and their leaves for healing."

What a lovely picture! As the river pursued its way, it attracted growth on its banks. Many trees flourished, their roots reaching deep into the riverbed as they drew nourishment from its waters. Such fruitfulness does not cease, and it does not wane when youth gives way to age. This is brought out also in Psalms 1:1–3, a picture of the perennial freshness of soul that can be maintained through the journey of life, because "the water for them flows from the sanctuary."

The Lord Jesus told us, in John 15:16, ". . . I have chosen you, and ordained you, that ye should go and bring forth fruit, and that your fruit should remain. . . ." This experience is no mere emotional upheaval, but an increasing fruitfulness displayed in growing Christlikeness.

The fullness of the Holy Spirit is a crisis followed by a process. An initial recognition of need opens the eyes of a believer to a totally new plane of Christian living, in which Christ is his all in all. As he by faith appropriates that life, he can begin to apply it in every detail of living, testing every problem, every misunderstanding, every blow from the enemy. So in every moment there can be victory—if he deliberately refuses to display his self-life and chooses, instead, to display the Lord Jesus. To such a Christian life others are attracted, for Jesus Christ said that if He is exalted, He will draw men to Him—and how is He exalted except through His people?

Not only is there fruitfulness through the river's flow, but also healing: ". . . Their fruit will be for food, and their leaves for healing."

There is no experience in life where the Christian has not a ministry of healing. The most unhappy home, the most damaging misunderstanding in the church fellowship, the most bitter and violent society, the most pervasive evil in daily living—*all* may be transformed by the Lord's sweetness and fragrance. Luther once said, "If you want to clean out a dunghill, turn the river Elbe into it!" How much do you want cleansing and healing for your life, your home, your church, and your neighborhood?

But you may say, "What can *I* do? I am so insignificant!"

All the Lord looks for is a channel through which He can flow in healing power. It must be a clean channel, open to the fullness of the Spirit and free from all impurity, which could clog the flow. Ask Him to make you willing to be such a channel by His power and for His glory, and He will answer that prayer in and through you.

Will you accept His offer of living water? Live in the presence of the Lord, in the power of His fullness, and allow Him to fill you with His Holy Spirit.

9

Facing the Climb

A mountaineer, contemplating a climbing expedition, will not rush into planning. This may take months, or even years. A group will study the peak to be conquered from every angle, then consult all the books written about it, and consider all the lessons learned by previous expeditions. To the best of human ability, risks and dangers will be recognized, and the group will have some idea of the challenge that faces them.

In the same way, a Christian learns from the lives and experiences of all who have walked that path before him, from New Testament times to his own generation. Let us study the life of a man who is, in my judgment, one of the most neglected figures in Scripture—John the Baptist. This man's ministry was revolutionary. His testimony to the Lord Jesus was unequaled in its depth and penetration, and the testimony of Christ concerning him was unsurpassed in its commendation—yet how little we hear or read concerning him. As we focus our attention upon his ministry, we will see its significance for these days.

We will consider his biography from three different angles: *the man and his message*—his testimony to his fellowmen; *the man and his Master*—his testimony to the Lord Jesus Christ; *the man and his merit*—the testimony Christ gave concerning him.

The worth of any man's ministry must be assessed against the background of the world in which he lived and the conditions under which he ministered.

The context of John's ministry is outlined in Luke 3:1, 2, where we find an imposing list of dignitaries—one emperor, one governor, three tetrarchs (satellite governors), and two high priests. It seems that the Spirit of God was drawing attention to a situation that was utterly impossible to break through: world dominion under the political dictatorship of Rome.

At this particular time poor little Israel, God's chosen nation, was under heavy bondage. Worse than that, it had a disgracefully corrupt priesthood. Politically and spiritually, the Jews were a downtrodden and divided people. It was then that God chose to introduce His spiritual kingdom. The whole world seemed to be spiritually hopeless, yet God could never run out of ideas or out of men. He always has His man for the hour.

At such a time, ". . . the word of God came unto John the son of Zacharias in the wilderness" (Luke 3:2). When God was about to do something, He brought to our attention the men who were at the top of the religious and political world, but then He bypassed them to empower a man prepared by Himself for the task.

"The word of God came unto John" really means "it came *upon* him." He was not aware merely of the world pressures under which he was living; he was also conscious of pressure from heaven. Our hope is not in a theological degree, but in the living God! This is the qualification for all preaching and witnessing: The word of God comes *upon* a man.

It came upon Jeremiah: ". . . I will make my words in thy mouth fire . . ." (Jeremiah 5:14). Perhaps you go through your Bible once a year, but has the Bible begun to go through you? Has the pressure of God's Word come upon you? Does it burn like fire in your bones? It is good to prepare and study for the ministry and to witness for Christ, but it is vital that you should realize you are helpless to influence anybody for God until He sends you out to burn and shine for Jesus.

John the Baptist lived at a strategic time in history. When the kingdom of God was about to dawn, he stood as a herald to proclaim the coming King. I believe we, too, are here on earth at a strategic time in history and that we are called upon to witness to Christ at the very dawn of His earthly reign. John preached at a time when God's people were in bondage spiritually, morally, and politically; we also live in such a time as that.

I do not know when the church has been so well equipped with so many things, yet so powerless to make an impact for God. We have lost touch with this generation of young people—95 percent of the people in Britain do not care what happens on Sundays in our churches—but the biggest tragedy of all is that we have lost touch with God. Never has the church had so much potential, but never has she been so paralyzed. Never has she been so called upon to speak with urgency and authority on matters of race, sex, drugs, and morality, but never has she been so silent. Never has there been a time when the church has been so called upon to display her oneness, but never has she been so divided, in spite of all the talk of unity.

By oneness, I do not mean a massive world church. There is a great difference between unity and uniformity, and the latter does not interest me very much. A man's label never troubles me, nor do I bother about the pond in which he fishes. But if there is a man anywhere who knows the Lord Jesus, who has been born from above, and into whose life the Holy Spirit has come with power, then that man is my brother, and I owe him my love. If I may say so, no matter how difficult it is for him, he also owes me his!

That is the true church, but never has that church been so divided as it is today. Surely the spectrum of evangelicalism everywhere is tragic indeed. Thank God for areas in which the Holy Spirit is mightily at work, but what about the attitude, for example, of the ultra-Calvinist to the charismatic movement? And vice versa, of course. What about the attitude of Evangelicals outside denominational lines to those who stay in them?

We are all brethren in Christ, but alas, suspicion, coldness, and even antagonism are too often evident. Never has the church needed so much as she does now a baptism of Holy Spirit love. We cannot possibly communicate life to the unsaved until we learn to share in openhearted fellowship with each other. That will call for brokenhearted repentance, which we, who profess to love the Lord but fail to love one another, have never known.

Surely it is time for the King to be announced.

It was a similar time when the Lord sent His messenger—and I wonder if He has today. Is there a John the Baptist anywhere upon whom the word of God has come? While multitudes perish and a whole generation goes out into a lost eternity, while we play games and discuss uniformity, is there a man upon whom the word of God has come with authority? While Satan throws dust in our eyes and confuses us about the issue, getting us to fight each other instead of fighting the real enemy, is there a man upon whom the word of God has come, who will bring us to repentance? Would to God such a man would emerge!

This, then, was the context of John's ministry. Here we see the relevance of it, for into a situation that was apparently hopeless from every angle, God moved. He bypassed all recognized authority to choose a hermit in the wilderness.

The content of John's message was quite devastating: "And he came into all the country about Jordan, preaching the baptism of repentance for the remission of sins" (Luke 3:3). John could not, of course, grant remission of sin, but he preached repentance as an attitude that would allow God to work.

I believe in the sovereignty of God in any situation, with absolute certainty that His purposes will be fulfilled. But there are some things that only God can do, and there are some things that only *I* can do and only *you* can do. Only God can save and redeem us; only God can sanctify us. But only *I* can repent; only *you* can believe. God will not do our repenting for us. John preached repentance as a heart condition in answer to which if these people were ready, then—dare I say it?—God was bound to work.

Then John the Baptist quoted from Isaiah 40: ". . . Prepare ye the way of the Lord, make his paths straight" (Luke 3:4). That word *straight* is the same as the word used by the apostle Peter to Simon the sorcerer, who sought to buy the Holy Spirit with money: ". . . Your heart is not *right* before God" (Acts 8:21 RSV). In other words, John was saying, "The kingdom of heaven is at hand; therefore, get right with God!"

There was an almost terrifying urgency in John's ministry. He passionately desired that this people might yet become a highway for God. The Jews thought that the coming of God's kingdom would bring them the privilege of ruling the heathen, but the truth of the matter was that it would mean their submission to the rule of God. Not their rule over others, but God's rule over them. John's call rings like an alarm bell in the soul: "Become a highway for our God! Make his paths straight! For all flesh shall see the salvation of our God."

Look at Luke 3:5, "Every valley shall be filled. . . ." That is the first big obstacle in the way of the King, for He cannot come while there are valleys, which demand clambering down hills, crossing streams, climbing up mountains. Tremendous valleys have to be filled to make His paths straight.

Think about the unfilled valleys in your life. What about the lack of planned waiting upon God? How many hours do you waste—

while you excuse yourself that you are too busy on the hectic conveyor-belt of this modern world? It is recorded of David that he sat before the Lord and opened his heart to Him. It takes time to do that, but alas, how many of us have the unfilled valley of no time to sit before God and talk with Him?

". . . Every mountain and hill shall be brought low. . . ." Is there some mountain in your life that bars the way to spiritual maturity and almost laughs at your search for holiness and God? It may be the mountain of pride and self-will, but whatever it is, the promise is that *every* mountain and hill shall be made low.

". . . The crooked shall be made straight, and the rough ways shall be made smooth." As I read those words, I have to ask myself, has my life in Christ made me straight, really? Is my word my bond? Have the rough places been made smooth? How often people see and touch the harshness, the rudeness and uncouthness of a Christian life, even though that person professes to be an evangelical believer! We are supposed to be stepping-stones to Christ, and a stepping-stone is designed to be walked upon. Some of us do not like being walked on. When that happens, we show all the roughness of an undisciplined, immature Christian life.

That is where repentance comes in—not just being sorry about something, but a change of mind that leads to a change of behavior. In other words, repentance is being sorry enough to stop! Many times I have preached repentance to an unconverted congregation that was not even there! "Repent and be saved" was the Gospel message, I believed, until the Lord showed me that the Christian life demands from us all a daily attitude of repentance.

I do not mean to suggest that there is no victory in Christ. Of course there is, but there is also an increasing sensitivity to what sin really is. That is a mark of growth in spiritual experience day by day. Do we now put the label SIN where we might not have placed it five years ago? As I try to walk more closely to Christ, I find myself more conscious of the need to repent. Is your repentance up-to-date, a constant change of mind toward sin that leads to a change of behavior?

As the Jews flocked to hear John the Baptist, they met with a scathing challenge:

> . . . O generation of vipers, who hath warned you to flee from the wrath to come? Bring forth therefore fruits worthy

of repentance, and begin not to say within yourselves, We have Abraham to our father: for I say unto you, That God is able of these stones to raise up children unto Abraham. And now also the axe is laid unto the root of the trees: every tree therefore which bringeth not forth good fruit is hewn down, and cast into the fire.

Luke 3:7–9

Neither would this be popular preaching today! John said, "Do not talk about repentance, but reveal it through your actions. Do not trust in your tradition, in your background or denomination, because the truth of God will show up the hypocrisy in your hearts."

John's message came to those religious leaders who thought they were least in need of it. It comes today with shattering authority from heaven to people who think they are least in need of it, to the spiritual hierarchy of the day, the "cream" of the church. It came to the Jews from a man outside their walls, a man God found in the wilderness.

Then they asked John what they should do. It is wonderful when a congregation realizes that they have to reach a verdict. Three times over in this passage John is asked, "What shall we do?" Here is a foretaste of what happened at Pentecost. If only we could hear people crying out these words today! Maybe that lack indicates something is wrong, not so much with the congregation, but with the preacher.

It is no sign of spiritual maturity to chat over the message with a friend, then rush off to get Sunday dinner. Here were people gripped by the words of a man who had the message burning in his heart, "Repent!"

"How? What are we to do?"

Notice what John said in reply: that repentance should be evidenced in the realm of economics. Your repentance will affect your attitude toward your wages, your hours of work; in fact, it will affect every relationship in life. Your repentance will reveal you as one whom God has broken and through whom He is revealing Himself in His supreme attribute, love. ". . . He that hath two coats, let him impart to him that hath none; and he that hath meat, let him do likewise" (Luke 3:11).

Paul summed up the whole concept in 1 Corinthians 13:1:

"Though I speak with the tongues of men and of angels, and have not charity, I am become as sounding brass, or a tinkling cymbal."

John appeared at a time when the Jews' situation seemed completely hopeless. But the key to new life lay with the people's willingness to repent of the deadness of their religion, to change their minds and their actions so that the love of God might be shed abroad.

John's message is as relevant now as it was when he first preached it. What we need today is orthodoxy on fire; we need to let God's Word burn in our hearts and make Jesus real. God help us to recognize the absolute inadequacy of "playing church." When at last He finds a company of people who are ready to come to grips with Him, *then* His Holy Spirit can move in.

When God chose a messenger, where did He find John? In the wilderness. But how did he get there?

John, the son of the priest Zacharias, was born into the priesthood. No doubt he pondered long on the message of the angel at his birth: "For he shall be great in the sight of the Lord, and shall drink neither wine nor strong drink; and he shall be filled with the Holy Ghost, even from his mother's womb" (Luke 1:15). In this way he ". . . grew, and waxed strong in spirit, and was in the deserts till the day of his shewing unto Israel" (Luke 1:80). Thus he was brought up in the awareness of God's purpose for his life, and at a certain point he headed off to be alone that he might think about all it involved.

Lovingly, let me say to you that no man ever speaks with authority who lives only among crowds. He must learn to see that crowd from a place where he is alone with God. John the Baptist, shut up with God in the wilderness, with a startling message burning in his soul, yielded to God's plan. "He will be great before the Lord," was the prophecy he fulfilled.

Many people want to be great in the sight of men, but it takes something else to be great in the sight of God. When we get to heaven, some people who have been very prominent here will be overshadowed by some saint of God, never heard in public, who will be revealed as great in the sight of the Lord!

"He shall drink no wine nor strong drink." John was to be temperate in his habits and keep his body in subjection. God's plan for his life was that he should be separated, filled with Holy Spirit power, invaded and possessed by God. Such was God's messenger, living in the wilderness away from the religious trappings of his day, alone with God to do His will.

God sent Moses into the desert for forty years, until He molded him as He wanted him. Have you spent even one day before the Lord, saying, "Lord, what has been Your real purpose for my life? How far short am I coming of Your plan?"

Can you really be God's messenger in such an hour as we live in? Will you be great in His sight because your life is temperate and you have certain standards? Have you willingly separated yourself from sin unto God, and are you now subject to Him? It is only through such subjection and discipline that you may experience His power in your life day by day. May your prayer always be, "Lord, make me such a person as that!"

10

The Place of the Leader

When a major mountaineering expedition is formed to conquer, let us say, one of the Himalayan peaks, every member of the team is chosen very carefully, but the supreme choice is that of the leader. He must be a very special person. On the one hand, he has to command authority, while at the same time he must have the ability to delegate responsibility. It is his task to lay the initial plans, to see that the track is as straightforward as possible and the supplies are adequate, and to maintain the morale of his team.

Every man on the team has to acknowledge in his heart and behavior that he recognizes the authority of the leader. As on such occasions those who make up mountaineering teams (and many similar ones) are strong-minded and individualistic, they have to do much heart searching before they accept a place in the team. Do they truly acknowledge their leader and trust his judgment? Will they follow him into places of extreme danger and remain loyal to him? These initial personal assessments are vital to any expedition, especially when life can be at risk, for any unsuitable team member or an inadequate leader could bring real disaster upon the whole operation.

There are a number of ways in which one can assess someone's leadership quality. His sincerity may be tested, but found sincerely wrong. His orthodoxy may be assessed, but he may be right in head knowledge and wrong in heart experience.

Perhaps the most important assessment to be made about any of us concerns the position we give our Leader, the Lord Jesus Christ. That is what matters most in public ministry and personal witness. When we have spoken in testimony or in a message, are our listeners merely impressed with our cleverness, with the brilliance of our intellect and oratory, or have we left behind the sweetness and fragrance of Christ Himself?

If we apply this supreme test to John the Baptist, he comes out triumphantly. So now let us consider the testimony he bore to Christ.

John the Baptist spoke of Christ as supreme in His power:

> "I baptize you with water for repentance, but he who is coming after me is mightier than I, whose sandals I am not worthy to carry; he will baptize you with the Holy Spirit and with fire. His winnowing fork is in his hand, and he will clear his threshing floor and gather his wheat into the granary, but the chaff he will burn with unquenchable fire."
>
> Matthew 3:11, 12 RSV

In this graphic statement there is exposed a vast difference between the ministry of John and the ministry of Jesus. John could only deal with the external, symbolized by water. But Jesus dealt with fire, which burns everything: the fire of the baptism of the Holy Spirit, burning out sin and burning in holiness.

Matthew 3:10–12 has three references to fire: In verse 10, fire consumes the fruitless tree that has been cut down. In verse 12, fire burns up the chaff that the fan has whirled away from the threshing floor. Verse 11 speaks of the fiery baptism of the Holy Spirit, which John said only Jesus can give, and which brings cleansing and life.

In Scripture, fire is often used as a symbol of the divine energy of God. When God made a covenant with Abraham concerning the land He had promised to him (*see* Genesis 15:17–21), fire passed between the parts of the sacrifice, as a token of His presence, a divine sealing of the pact that this land was to be completely possessed by the people of God.

After the Lord had trained Moses for forty years in the desert, to take the self-importance from him, He spoke to him about delivering Israel. God spoke from a bush that blazed with the flame of His presence, but was not consumed. This was the symbol of God's government over a nation yet to be delivered. Again, when the people of Israel left Egypt behind and journeyed through the wilderness, God sent a pillar of fire to guide them.

Fire, therefore, symbolized divine energy, the grace and guidance of God. Such was to be the work of Jesus Christ: to come upon a group of people with a baptism that would ignite dead, earthy material into a flame of warmth and love. When the Holy Spirit came at Pentecost, He came in the form of tongues of flame.

Fire! It symbolized God's desire to reveal His grace in your life. His government and guidance are expressed in the words, "He will baptize you with the Holy Ghost and with fire." The man who submits completely to the government of God knows the infilling of the Spirit of God. Day by day he will experience the grace and guidance of God. In other words, for him the Lord Jesus is always sufficient.

A prominent businessman in South Africa ordered a Rolls Royce car, with which he was immensely impressed. One day he went to the car dealer and asked him what its horsepower was. The dealer said that the Rolls Royce company never stated the horsepower of their engines. The businessman specifically asked the dealer to find out. Because the man was an important customer, the dealer sent a long cable to the Rolls Royce works in Derby, England, setting out the exact specifications of the engine, asking them to cable immediately the exact horsepower. Shortly the reply arrived, bearing one word: ADEQUATE!

On a stiff climb, one's equipment is either adequate or not adequate—there is no room for error.

I am glad to speak from my heart concerning a Savior whom I find to be adequate. In some measure, out of my own personal experience, I know the fire of the grace of God, the government of God, and the guidance of God in my life. When the supply is adequate, one needs nothing further!

Only Jesus Christ is completely adequate. He said, "I am come to send fire on the earth . . ." (Luke 12:49). On the day of Pentecost, Peter proclaimed it: "Therefore being by the right hand of God exalted, and having received of the Father the promise of the Holy Ghost, he hath shed forth this, which ye now see and hear" (Acts 2:33).

The Holy Spirit came not in answer to a ten-day prayer meeting by 120 people in an upper room, but in answer to the prayer of the Lord Jesus, who said to His disciples before He went to the cross, "I will pray the Father, and he shall give you another Comforter, that he may abide with you for ever" (John 14:16).

Christ had ascended to the right hand of the Father, entering heaven as a man, the first man ever to reach there by His own holiness and goodness, needing none to intercede for Him. He stood before the throne of God, and His presence in human form made a demand upon God the Father, for here was God's perfect Man in the glory. God met the demand, pouring out at Pentecost the same Spirit who had filled His Son all His earthly life, that the Spirit might fill Christ's Body here on earth. God meant that the work Jesus began should be developed and brought to a climax by His church here below.

The Holy Spirit has come into our hearts, therefore, as an eternal principle of life, cleansing, sanctifying, and freeing us from the cold starchiness of churchianity. His presence delivers us from the sham of dutiful church attendance. The Spirit fills us with the sheer thrill of the presence of Christ in our everyday living. Hallelujah!

But alas, to so many Christians, Christ is not real. They repeat the words of the creed, "I believe in God the Father Almighty . . . and in Jesus Christ, the only-begotten Son," but as a living companion who thrills and fills their lives seven days a week, He just is not a reality.

The reality of Christ in our lives is, I believe, our most desperate need today. Why doesn't it happen? I think when we sift out the secondary concerns, there are two basic reasons.

First, we are afraid. We see about us so much confusion and uncertainty. We have exchanged the false fire of fanaticism for the no fire of orthodoxy, and we are pillars of ice. What we need is orthodoxy on fire and doctrines coming alive, but we are fearful of the consequences.

Second, perhaps God cannot take His children seriously because we do not take Him seriously enough. We can have as much of Jesus as we want; we get no more and no less. Our lives are brimming over with our pressures, problems, cares and the indulgences of an affluent society. We crowd out the Holy Spirit and grieve Him. We remain content with the baptism of water, the external ministry of John. It may take a furnace of tribulation to separate today's church from the dead forms of religious activity that we regard as normal.

In our culture, so often we settle down and cling to the ways in which things have been done for generations, losing the fire and enthusiasm and reality of the Risen Lord. We must recapture it! Unless we do, Matthew 3:12 tells us that He, Jesus, will burn up the chaff with unquenchable fire.

I say this solemnly: Either we will know the fire of the Holy Spirit in our lives today and the continuing guidance of the Lord who is alive and real to us, or one day we will experience another kind of fire, which tries every man's work and consumes the chaff (*see* 1 Corinthians 3:13). Only one thing will survive God's testing fire: the life of the Spirit of God in us.

In your daily experience, is Jesus supreme in His power over your life? Do you know the fire in your heart today, making Jesus real to you? If you are cold and you see a fire, you can choose whether or not to warm yourself. Move over to the fire, and inevitably you catch the glow. Stay away from it, and you remain cold. Similarly, you can choose to live near Christ, catch the glow, and burn for Him, or stand apart in the cold, although you remain an orthodox believer.

But when you draw near the fire, you cannot control the consequences. You cannot stand near the fire and remain cold; you cannot stay away from the fire and be warm. If you say in your heart and mean it, "Lord, give me the power of the Holy Spirit for life and witness," and stay close to Him, you will find that the fire begins to glow in you. Jesus alone can warm you with His Spirit, for He is supreme in His power.

The second thrilling message in John's testimony was that Christ is supreme in His person. "The next day John seeth Jesus coming unto him, and saith, Behold the Lamb of God, which taketh away the sin of the world" (John 1:29).

John admitted that he did not know who Jesus was until God told him: "And I knew him not: but he that sent me to baptize with water, the same said unto me, Upon whom thou shalt see the Spirit descending, and remaining on him, the same is he which baptizeth with the Holy Ghost" (John 1:33). In a blaze of revelation, John announced, "Behold the Lamb of God!"

Long before, as Isaac and Abraham went together up Mount Moriah, Isaac asked his father, "Where is the lamb for a burnt offering?" His father answered, "God will provide himself a lamb" (*see* Genesis 22:7, 8).

Isaiah had written, ". . . He is brought as a lamb to the slaughter, and as a sheep before her shearers is dumb, so he openeth not his mouth" (53:7).

John was the first to introduce the new song of the angels in heaven:

Worthy the Lamb that died, they cry,
  To be exalted thus;
Worthy the Lamb, our lips reply,
  For He was slain for us.

See Revelation 5:9

Not only was Jesus the Lamb of God, but John the Baptist stated, "And I saw, and bare record that this is the Son of God" (John 1:34). When John saw the Holy Spirit descend on Jesus at His baptism, he knew Jesus was the only begotten Son of the Father, exalted in majesty and glory. With that revelation came John's confession to the genuineness of Jesus, the assurance that He was indeed the Messiah, the Anointed of God.

Later there was a moment when John the Baptist doubted Him. Look at the record in Matthew 11:3. John was in prison, persecuted by Herod for daring to criticize his relationship with his brother's wife. Through his followers, John sent a message to Jesus, "Art thou He that should come, or do we look for another?"

John the Baptist sat in a dungeon, while outside, in the palace, Herodias hated him with all her power and waited for her opportunity to kill him. News reached John of what Jesus was doing—and not doing, too, for there was no sign of His setting up a kingdom. *Can it be He after all?* thought John. *Here I am in prison for my loyalty to God's truth, and does He care?*

That brings John very near to us in experience. Perhaps you feel sometimes that no deliverance has been sent from heaven, and you question God's concern for you. I have always wondered why the Lord never chose John the Baptist to be a disciple and why He allowed him to be beheaded. He allowed the apostle James to be killed, but his brother John lived to a ripe old age.

While there was no deliverance for Herod's prisoner, there was a word from the Master: "Go and shew John again those things which ye do hear and see...," and a warning, "blessed is he, whosoever shall not be offended in me" (Matthew 11:4, 6). John was probably disappointed, for he had expected a revival similar to that in the days of Elijah.

Do you have a controversy with God? Perhaps you expected healing, but you have not had it. You may have financial difficulties, and the whole honor of God on your behalf seems to be at stake. Whatever your circumstance, the situation remains unaltered. Nobody ever says, because of your life and testimony, "What must I do to be saved?" You are weary of being an apparently fruitless Christian.

Jesus has a word for you: "Happy is he who is not offended in Me." One day He will explain, but until then, what you cannot understand of His ways, you must simply trust to Him.

John's testimony emerged triumphant through his doubt and despair; does yours? People who will not come inside our churches will watch how we react when we go through times of darkness and doubt. Even if the bottom has fallen out of your world, look up by faith to your Lord and say, ". . . I know whom I have believed, and am persuaded that he is able to keep that which I have committed unto him . . ." (2 Timothy 1:12).

John testified that Christ was the Lamb of God and the Son of God. Although we also may be called to pass through trials, ill health, and suffering, He is still the Lord who has never allowed anyone to pluck a single little lamb out of His hand.

Yet another chord in the harmony of John's testimony to his Master was that Christ is supreme in His position. Notice how this rugged preacher bent low before the Lord Jesus: ". . . He who is coming after me is mightier than I, whose sandals I am not worthy to carry . . ." (Matthew 3:11 RSV). John implied that he was not even worthy to be the slave of his Master, an attitude that spells out to me that Christ had been put on the throne of John's life.

There are people like that today. In Leslie Lyall's book, *The Wind of Change,* published by the Overseas Missionary Fellowship, which describes the first ten years under communism in China, he tells the story of a girl to whom the communists came with handcuffs to take her off to prison, and perhaps torture and death. As they approached she held out her hands, saying, "I am not worthy."

I wonder if it will take persecution to awaken us in the West, so that we come to that attitude. In John 3:30 John the Baptist said, "He must increase, but I must decrease." Christ enthronement means self-effacement. He must grow while I get smaller—and that is a very unpopular concept these days.

Look finally at John 1:37—what an amazing verse that is! "And the two disciples heard him [John the Baptist] speak, and they followed Jesus." I have written beside that verse, "Lord, make this true of my ministry!" But am I really sure? It is nice to be able to talk about *my* congregation, *my* people, *my* work—to head up a little group and feel they are mine. How wonderful, though, to speak to people and through the testimony find them following Jesus, even if they leave one's own little group.

John the Baptist was concerned about taking himself out of the picture and making Christ the center. Self-effacement and Christ enthronement were the secrets of his ministry.

Such was his testimony to his Master. What about yours and mine?

The supremacy of the person of Christ—the Lamb of God, the Son of God—is only theory until it blots me out of the picture altogether and I recognize Him to be supreme. Only when He is enthroned will the fire of the Spirit warm my life, and then men will not look to me, but will follow Jesus.

That is why an experience of the Holy Spirit that does not make Jesus precious to you is not valid. But any experience of the Spirit of God that brings to you the sufficiency of His grace, the reality of His government, and the consciousness of His guidance, is the real fire, which gives a glow that makes people want to follow—not you, but Him, for we are on His team, and He is our divine Leader.

11

The Place of the Follower

What made John the Baptist the kind of man he was? Not by any stretch of the imagination was he a man on a pedestal, but someone who was chosen by God for a significant ministry prior to the coming of Christ. In these days, God is looking for the same kind of man to be a herald of the coming of the King.

I am not quite sure how many Christians have really been stabbed awake to the fact that the time is shorter than we may think. Never did we imagine that in the West we would have such a society of violence and crime, drug and alcohol addiction, and other ills. We thought that our Christian background would prevent this, but it is a broken dike.

These crisis days require a crisis ministry. The Church must awaken and face up to this issue—each one of us individually— for it has never been so important as now to consider what should be the personal witness of each Christian.

What kind of men and women does God intend us to be? What can we learn from John the Baptist and his impact upon his own time and place?

If you want a true appraisal of a person, to whom would you turn? The only One whose assessment can be completely accurate is the Lord Jesus Christ. Approval by the Lord is the only thing that matters, ultimately. I want always to live as one who does not regard the praise or blame of others, but whose concern is to be pleasing to Him. What, then, was Jesus' appraisal of John the Baptist? As we answer that question, of course, we can see what kind of person God is looking for in this twentieth century to be a herald for our coming Lord.

In Luke 7:24 we find first what Jesus said about the grandeur of the man. ". . . What went ye out into the wilderness for to see? A reed shaken with the wind?"

After the messengers of John departed, Jesus began to speak to the people about him. The timing is worth noting, I think. When other people praise us to our face, very often they criticize us behind our back, but the Lord did the reverse. He always faced people with their faults.

The first thing Jesus said about John the Baptist was that he was a man of rocklike steadiness, or firmness. ". . .What went ye out into the wilderness for to see? A reed shaken with the wind?" No, indeed! John the Baptist was not a man uncertain of himself, blown about by every wind of theory. He was not always looking for some new thing or some new experience, nor was he afraid to stand up and be counted. John was sure of his message, sure of his calling, sure of his Lord. In John 1:6 it is stated that John the Baptist was ". . . a man sent from God . . ." and he knew it.

I believe it is the prerogative of every Christian to have this certainty in his heart, every day of his life, that he has been sent by God. It is no accident that we are alive in such a day as this. Wherever we are placed, we are there because God put us there. It is no greater thing to be a preacher than to be a businessman or a housewife who is in that place because God put him or her there.

John the Baptist was a man sent from God. That touched his lips with authority and provided in his life an atmosphere of assurance in every situation. The call of God was behind him, the need of people before him, and therefore he was steady.

If our grasp of doctrine and truth is only superficial and intellectual, we will convince nobody. But if God's truth has gripped our lives and our whole being is yielded in obedience to it, then it becomes an irresistible power in our hearts, and our lives convey something of heavenly steadiness.

My friend George Duncan has written a book entitled *Mastery in the Storm*. That is what we need! Many people are fine Christians when everything is going well, but when a storm comes, they press the panic button just like any unbeliever. They go completely to pieces and resign or run away. How many of God's people allow the storms of life to drive them from God instead of to Him? How many fail to realize that the disasters that come into every life are sent by God Himself?

No matter what storm, pressure, or problem confronts you at this moment, it has not come to you without first having passed through the presence of God, and it reached you by His permission. He has allowed it to prove the reality of your faith. Can you be steady in the storm? Or do you have a flash of enthusiasm for a few weeks, then when things get hard, you give in?

The Lord today needs men who are steady because, believe me, the storm is here. I do not think the West has ever faced such pressure internally as it is experiencing now. The Christian Church, a little remnant, but the true Body of Christ, needs to stand up and be counted. They must be prepared to stand for Christian morality and truth; they must recognize that only righteousness exalts a nation, and sin is a rebuke to any people (*see* Proverbs 14:34). If you stand up for righteousness in this day and age, you will find yourself in the midst of a storm!

If you have children in school, university, or college, you know what they have to face. I think Christian young people need a tremendous share in our prayers. They find themselves in situations where everything evil is offered them and Christian fellowship is scarce. They need to have that rocklike firmness, prepared to be unashamed of their Lord and defend His name. They can too easily be blown about by every pressure and blast that is brought upon them.

Further, John was a man of absolute self-denial: "But what went ye out for to see? A man clothed in soft raiment? . . ." (Luke 7:25). John was utterly indifferent to material things. His home was a desert, and his clothing was appropriate to it. Instead of adorning and pampering himself, he subjected himself completely. He came to announce a rejected Messiah, and he lived like a man in exile. He knew there was no vacation from his vocation. No self-indulgent man could ever shake a nation for God; if there is the least suspicion that a Christian leader is self-serving, then at once his power is nullified.

In my younger days, when I was playing football, I learned what it was to discipline myself. Up early in the morning to run, before going to my office. After a hard day at the desk, off to the nearest running track to run for another hour, then skip and do other exercises. Back at my rooming house, I changed into my football strip, and putting one shoulder against the corner of the house wall, I would push and push. Then I would do the same on the other side, until my body was aching. But I was determined that when I turned out to play on Saturdays, anyone tackling me would come in contact with a lump of concrete and would be discouraged from repeating his daring!

Believe me, when I went week by week to play, I was as fit and tough as anyone could be. In the physical realm at that time my activities paralleled what Paul described in 1 Corinthians 9:27 (TLB), "Like an athlete I punish my body, treating it roughly, training it to do what it should, not what it wants to. Otherwise I fear that after enlisting others for the race, I myself might be declared unfit and ordered to stand aside."

Yes, John the Baptist was truly a man of self-denial and disciplined habits, but those words are not very popular today, are they?

Let me bear testimony: I never have to use an alarm clock. I can go to bed at night and say, "Now, Lord, I want to be awake tomorrow morning at six," and, sure enough, I am awake. But I tell you this: the Lord *wakes* me up, but He doesn't *get* me up! *I* have to get "blanket victory"—out of bed and on my knees—and thus discipline my life.

Maybe you are active in Christian work—a deacon, Sunday-school teacher, on this or that committee—and doing a tremendous job. Bless you for the work you do! But I tell you this: When you substitute *doing* things for *being* somebody, you are in grave danger. God wants quality people, people of absolute self-denial, people who know this is a body of sin and that the devil has a foothold in it. Satan is always attacking the Christian, and he always will, until we get into heaven. Therefore we must be able to say no to ourselves and yes to Jesus Christ. John was a man like that, and only that kind of person can accomplish anything for God today.

Notice, too, that John was a man of unusual prophetic insight: "But what went ye out for to see? A prophet? Yea, I say unto you, and much more than a prophet" (Luke 7:26). John was a voice crying in the wilderness, a voice sent from God, and his authority was recognized. He was not just the echo of someone else's voice; he had a firsthand message from heaven, and even the dullest people realized his authenticity.

There are too many echoes around today; God wants men and women who will be voices. Paul said, "For I have received of the Lord that which I also delivered unto you ..." (1 Corinthians 11:23), and no preacher has any right to stand in a pulpit if he cannot say that. No one giving witness or testimony, no Sunday-school teacher or Bible-class leader has any right to address a group unless he stands as a voice. Western civilization desperately needs such voices today.

Conditions in John Wesley's day may have been very different, but in the book *England Before and After Wesley,* it is shown how he was used by God to save Britain from the revolution that France experienced at that time. John Wesley was a voice. Britain in those days was asleep and needed a voice to awaken her; Wesley was that voice. But Britain is not asleep today—she is drugged! She is intoxicated with sin, immorality, sexuality, and everything that is debasing. This situation needs something more: a voice of authority that will really reach the heart.

One of the most devastating battles in World War II was at the Anzio beachhead in Italy. While living in the States, I met an American who had fought at Anzio. His whole regiment had been practically wiped out; he was one of very few survivors.

He said to me, "The amazing thing about the situation was that we Americans and the Germans had exactly the same equipment. We were firing at each other from close quarters, yet our shells were bouncing off the German tanks, while every German shell was piercing our armor. Later we found out that engineers in Germany had discovered the secret of muzzle velocity, which means that the shell was made to spin at such speed that it could bore into and penetrate our tanks."

I am not pleading for noise in preaching, I am pleading for penetration, for some word that comes from God with shattering authority. Such was the voice of John the Baptist, a man of unusual prophetic insight.

Look again to see the glory of his message: ". . . Yea, I say unto you, and much more than a prophet. This is he, of whom it is written, Behold, I send my messenger before thy face, which shall prepare thy way before thee" (Luke 7:26, 27). "Before His face" means "immediately before Him." You see, the thing that made John great and gave him penetration and authority was something that is open to us all. It was his nearness to Christ.

Notice a significant phrase about him in John 5:35, where Jesus said, "He was a burning and a shining light. . . ." John was not a light in the sense that Christ was a light, but a luminary—a reflector of Jesus.

On a moonlight night you may exclaim, "How brightly the moon is shining!" But you would be wrong, because the moon cannot shine. The astronauts have confirmed that it is composed of lack-luster material, which has no capacity to shine. But as it orbits the earth, which orbits the sun, the moon reflects the sun's light and shines into the darkness of the world.

Writing to the Philippians, Paul said his prayer for them was "That ye may be blameless and harmless, the sons of God, without rebuke, in the midst of a crooked and perverse nation, among whom ye shine as lights in the world" (2:15).

John the Baptist was God's messenger, a luminary who had been with Christ and caught the glow and reality of His presence and had begun to reflect His beauty. So he burned as a light of God before the world. Have you caught the glow?

Although this generation might require new methods—and it is necessary to search for them in order to reach young people—there is nothing you can substitute for the glow of reflecting the Lord through a Christ-centered and Christ-controlled life.

"For I say unto you," Jesus declared in Luke 7:28. "Among those that are born of women there is not a greater prophet than John the Baptist. . . ."

Perhaps all that has been said about John has made you feel that he was a man apart. If so, then think of the gulf in his ministry: ". . . But he that is least in the kingdom of God is greater than he," Jesus continued.

Here the Lord introduced another standard of greatness. This greatest of all prophets, because he was the messenger chosen to announce the coming of Christ, had to give way to the wisdom and greatness of the smallest person in the kingdom of heaven. If you have the life of the King in your heart, then you are in the kingdom.

"Our Father, which art in heaven," Jesus taught us to pray. "Hallowed be Thy name: Thy kingdom come. . . ." This is not merely prophetic praying, but experiential praying: "Lord Jesus, set up Thy kingdom in my heart." We have been delivered from the kingdom of Satan into the kingdom of God, and from henceforth we are citizens of heaven. Earth is not our abiding kingdom. Our true kingdom and citizenship is in heaven, for we are children of the King of Glory.

Because this is true—and I hope this thought will amaze you as it did me when I realized it for the first time—you and I are closer to Jesus than John ever was! Although the Spirit of God was upon him, he never experienced the indwelling Holy Spirit, whom we have been privileged to receive. The very lowliest believer indwelt by the third Person of the Trinity knows more of Jesus and possesses a fuller spiritual life than John ever did.

This gulf was recognized by other people:

> Therefore they sought again to take him: but he [Jesus] escaped out of their hand, And went away again beyond Jordan into the place where John at first baptized; and there he abode. And many resorted unto him, and said, John did no miracle: but all things that John spake of this man were true. And many believed on him there.
>
> John 10:39–42

Christ had retreated momentarily from the crowd, with its pressure, and returned to the river Jordan. Many people followed Him there. Perhaps He reflected on His baptism and John's hesitancy, when he said, "I need to be baptized of Thee." Jesus' reply, "Suffer it to be so now," was followed by the voice from heaven saying, "This is My beloved Son." In spite of that, the verdict was, "John did no miracle." That puts him right alongside us—he did no miracle! No, but all things that he spoke concerning Jesus were true, and many believed on Him. That was all John could do: That was the limit of his power.

Christ said to His people, ". . . He that believeth on me, the works that I do shall he do also; and greater works that these shall he do; because I go unto my Father" (John 14:12). In the life that is committed to Christ, the prospect of "greater works" is not a far-off fantasy or an absurd proposition, but something that becomes a practical reality. By the Holy Spirit, the people of God could turn the tide of history.

You may ask what will be demanded of you in your ministry as a herald of the King. There are two requisites: consecration and crucifixion.

Consecration involves an absorption in the things of God; it means truth has taken fire in you. You no longer "play church"; you realize that the most important thing in life is to obey the Word of God. I am convinced that it is not a greater knowledge of doctrine that we need, but 100 percent obedience to what we know.

Consecration demands not only obedience, but sacrifice, when our purse is laid at Christ's feet as well as our heart. Once Britain was the chief missionary-sending nation; now she is the greatest gambling nation. God's people need to get back to the spirit of sacrifice that once made this nation great. We must not only take God seriously, but tell Him that we are prepared to be serious regarding all of His demands upon our lives.

The second requisite for the ministry of a herald like John the Baptist is crucifixion, putting the self-life to death. When Jesus saved us that was His purpose. Paul said, "But God forbid that I should glory, save in the cross of our Lord Jesus Christ, by whom the world is crucified unto me, and I unto the world.... From henceforth let no man trouble me: for I bear in my body the marks of the Lord Jesus" (Galatians 6:14, 17).

God will never anoint the self in us with power, but if we are prepared for that self to go to the cross, He replaces it with Jesus, and in Him there is all power.

For a herald sent by God, there will be commendation: "Well done, good and faithful servant." Well done, not well believed! It is what you have done with the life and power of Christ within you—your obedience to His will, not just your faith—that will receive commendation. What a day to live for!

But today we have the privilege of living as heralds of the King, being followers of our great Leader. Therefore let not the trumpet of our testimony have an uncertain sound, but be used to summon those at present outside the kingdom to know and love and worship the King, Jesus Christ our Lord.

12

A Stern Preparation

When a mountaineering expedition is announced, few people realize the months of preparation that are already under way. Equipment has to be tested, and above all, the physical, emotional, and mental reaction of every man in the expedition must be put to the most rigorous tests that can be devised. Practice climbs are made on every sort of terrain that might be encountered. Nothing is left to chance. Techniques must be perfected until they are performed automatically. The climbers face a stern preparation, but it is absolutely necessary, because slipshod training could result in accident and death.

As we turn to the story of the prophet Jonah, we find him undergoing a stern preparation in his training as a disciple. Jonah's book is unique, for it is not the record of his ministry, but rather of God's dealings with him. He may have been a moral coward, but it must have cost him a lot to write down this story; it could never have been written if he had not done so himself.

Jonah was one of the earlier prophets, ministering in the northern kingdom of Israel in the reign of Jeroboam II (*see* 2 Kings 14:24, 25). The Assyrians had captured much territory and were likely to take more, for Israel seemed powerless to withstand them. In this period of bitter affliction, Jonah became God's messenger of hope and salvation. In the Name of the Lord, Jonah declared that the coast would be restored to Israel. He believed God's Word and preached it faithfully.

Then God fulfilled His promise and saved Israel. So Jonah had been an effective servant of the Lord to Israel in a time of spiritual decline. This is an important background for the story contained in the book bearing Jonah's name. In case there are some who doubt its historical truth, I would point out that the Lord Jesus mentioned it as the only sign He would give to His own generation of His death and resurrection (*see* Matthew 12:38–41). His authentication should be enough for us.

However, my interest in this book is not so much for its history, but for its exposure of God's dealings with the inmost hearts of His people. The lengths to which God will go in order to achieve His purposes and the lengths to which *we* will go in shirking the cost of discipleship are all revealed here. It is amazing, the sheer pigheadedness of a man in the face of all God's goodness and mercy. Over this book I would write, "Lord, great is *my* stubbornness, but greater still is Thy faithfulness!"

There are only forty-eight verses in the four chapters of this book, but how many lessons there are for us to consider! Let us first look at Jonah 1:1–3 and see the disciple's rebellion:

> Now the word of the Lord came unto Jonah the son of Amittai, saying, Arise, go to Nineveh, that great city, and cry against it; for their wickedness is come up before me. But Jonah rose up to flee unto Tarshish from the presence of the Lord, and went down to Joppa; and he found a ship going to Tarshish: so he paid the fare thereof, and went down into it, to go with them unto Tarshish from the presence of the Lord.

"The word of the Lord *came* to Jonah"—what a solemn and awe-inspiring moment! God spoke as Jehovah, issuing orders that must be obeyed. What was the command? "Arise, go to Nineveh, that great city, and cry against it."

Nineveh was indeed a great city, a thousand years old in Jonah's day, founded by Nimrod (*see* Genesis 10:8–11). So why Nineveh? The answer is God's business, but He was concerned for the city, with the yearning of love. Unless the people repented, God must in justice judge it and destroy it. So He sought a messenger for a task very near to His heart in order to give the people of Nineveh a chance of salvation. Here is an Old Testament example of the great New Testament truth that "God so loved *the world* [not only Israel] that He gave. . . ."

Even more important than the salvation of Nineveh was the disciplining of Jonah. The prophet had to learn to obey God in a three-fold way: first, to turn aside from his popularity and success, at any cost walking the path of surrender; then to share in the compassion of God for people who were deadly enemies (as the Lord Jesus said many centuries later, to learn to love one's enemies); and also to take sides with God against sin.

There is a Nineveh to which God calls every one of us, not a far-off heathen city, perhaps, but more likely a nearby, familiar circumstance. It is the lesson, not the location, that counts. It is a place where we need to bow before God and die to self, a place where we must ally ourselves with God against sin, a place where all the things we count precious cannot be allowed to matter at all.

It is a place where the Lord and *His* will and desires matter supremely. Faithfulness to His will is the only issue, for the results are all in His hand. It is a place where we must be ready to be counted a failure, yet a place that leads to blessing beyond our wildest dreams, for the place of self-crucifixion is the only place of Holy Spirit anointing. If we seek to serve the Lord and respond in love to Him, this call to a training school of character comes to us. For only the person who is broken and filled with the Holy Spirit can be made like the Lord Jesus Himself, which is God's aim.

How did Jonah respond to this awesome summons? *"But* Jonah rose up to flee unto Tarshish."

God said, "Nineveh!" Jonah said, "Tarshish!" Here is the point at which he rebelled, but could he not stay where he was? No, that was impossible, for the word of the Lord was too insistent, and there was no silencing it. You have experienced that, haven't you? In the words of the Psalmist, "Day and night thy hand was heavy upon me; my strength was dried up as by the heat of summer. Selah" (Psalms 32:4 RSV).

In a vain attempt to get away from the pricks of conscience, Jonah fled from the presence of the Lord, as he thought. Tarshish was at the opposite end of the Mediterranean Sea from the route to Nineveh. Jonah was prepared to undertake all the hazards of a sea voyage and whatever might happen to him once he arrived at his destination. He was ready to risk anything in order to escape the presence of the Lord, which forced him to the responsibility of an unpleasant and costly task.

Possibly Jonah had heard that Tarshish was a prosperous and attractive place. Perhaps he thought, *I'll enjoy the material comforts, and it will be easy to forget this inner voice that keeps nagging at me.*

Maybe his thoughts were already turning to what he later wrote in Jonah 4:2, that he knew the Lord was merciful and would give this fearsome enemy an opportunity to repent. Jonah did not want that to happen, for if God spared them, they might become a greater danger to Israel. In Jonah's eyes, Nineveh deserved its punishment, not an opportunity to repent.

What a picture of the way God deals with His people even today! There is no silencing His voice as He calls us to take a stand against sin and to go to the place of crucifixion, trusting Him for the consequences. But are we willing for that? And even beyond our submission, are we willing to share the love in God's heart for the person who may be an enemy, that difficult person from whom we long to get away? God has to break us until our one desire is for that person's salvation.

We always prefer an easier road; we try to avoid the place of self-crucifixion. So we flee from the presence of the Lord, choosing comfort and material prosperity. Heaven watches as another servant, perhaps a potential instrument for Holy Spirit revival, who could shake a continent, rebels and refuses to pay the price. How the Lord's heart must break!

Following rebellion comes relegation, for now look at Jonah: he "went down to Joppa; and he found a ship going to Tarshish: so he paid the fare thereof, and went down into it . . ." (Jonah 1:3).

The devil always has a convenient ship ready for a man who is running away from God! Yes, and it is "travel now, pay later!" Jonah took an irrevocable step of disobedience; he paid the fare (it is always costly to disobey God) and went down into the ship.

Adam sinned, and it cost him Eden.

Saul disobeyed, and it cost him his kingdom.

Ananias sinned, and it cost him his life.

You and I have sinned—what has it cost?

Like Jonah, we think we can get rid of an unpleasant issue. Why should we tread the Calvary Road? Any other way seems much better. But we cannot get rid of God like that, as the Psalmist discovered.

> Whither shall I go from thy spirit? or whither shall I flee from thy presence? If I ascend up into heaven, thou art there: if I make my bed in hell, behold, thou art there. If I take the wings of the morning and dwell in the uttermost parts of the

sea; Even there shall thy hand lead me, and thy right hand shall hold me.

Psalms 139:7–10

Jonah had to find that out, and so will all of us. In the meantime, every step away from God took him *down:* down to Joppa, down to the ship, down into the inner part of the ship, and finally down into the ocean. That is true of all who refuse the cross: joy decreases, power vanishes, communion is lost, and peace departs. What a high price to pay!

Yet the Lord would not let Jonah go: His hand was still on the bridle. And as the bridle checks an obstinate animal and a whip chastises it, Jonah found that his own way led him lower and lower, to terror and almost to death.

After Jonah had refused God's still, small voice, the Lord had to take a megaphone to get his attention. "But the Lord sent out a great wind into the sea, . . . so that the ship was like to be broken" (Jonah 1:4). All this, but the one to whom God wanted to speak was fast asleep. His disobedience made him indifferent to danger and insensitive to the needs of others.

Yes, Jonah was relegated to uselessness, and how easily that can happen to any one of us. Jonah was hardened by indifference, helpless to pray, careless for souls, and blind to the damage his own stupidity had caused those who sailed with him. This was indeed a stern preparation for the Lord's service.

First, the sailors had to throw overboard many valuable things, but they found that the storm did not cease. When God revealed the truth of the situation to them, Jonah was unmasked. He had to acknowledge his faith in ". . . the Lord, the God of heaven, which hath made the sea and the dry land."

"What shall we do unto thee, that the sea may be calm unto us?" asked the terrified sailors.

Jonah replied, "Take me up, and cast me forth into the sea; so shall the sea be calm unto you" (*see* Jonah 1:5, 7, 9, 11, 12).

Strive as they would to bring the ship to land, the sailors found it of no avail, for "the sea . . . was tempestuous against them" (verse 13). There was only one way to still the storm. Jonah had to go overboard. A man of God out of the will of God is a menace to himself and to others.

Now put yourself into that picture. If you too have a controversy with the Lord over some "Nineveh," if your mad attempt to escape from God must stop, if the storm that has arisen in your life and in the lives of others because of your action is to grow calm, you must accept crucifixion and burial, like Jonah, and be flung into the ocean of Calvary. That sounds drastic, and it is, but you are also flung into the arms of the God who put the storm there to bring you closer to Himself.

A stern preparation, indeed, but it causes us to realize that God is always with us. He sees the end from the beginning and works toward His goal. No amount of hard rowing on our part will do, no amount of strenuous work or giving up precious things. Only one vital action is necessary—the self-life must be handed over to death. Think of the damage that has been done to other lives and to Christian work because of stubborn or ignorant refusal of this principle!

As God's grace always overflows in blessing, so His judgment overflows in punishment, because our sin causes others to suffer and therefore cannot possibly be condoned. So often, attempting to make up for our rebellion, we offer the Lord work, while He waits to accept a broken heart. Repentance is the only gateway to the fullness of His blessing. This crisis of identification with Jesus—will you face it?

In the roar of the tempest, your plunge into the cross will not be heard. There is never any public applause or cheers from the crowd, no press write-ups or headlines, but the effect will be seen in a mighty outpouring of blessing. ". . . And the sea ceased from her raging," we read in Jonah 1:15. What a victory in the Name of the Lord!

13

A Strange Reward

In the story of Jonah, we come to the portion that has been a debating ground for centuries. "Now the Lord had prepared a great fish to swallow up Jonah. And Jonah was in the belly of the fish three days and three nights" (Jonah 1:17).

In the previous chapter, we read how Jonah was aroused to the stupidity of his rebellion. He found that the only way back to peace with his God was through confession and repentance. When a man accepts the principle of death, what happens?

The Lord was waiting. He was not taken by surprise, for the hand of His judgment had been upon Jonah to bring him to that point. So He prepared a great fish to swallow him. This was not an act of punishment, but of preservation. The Lord always prepares a hospital for those He has to wound; on every occasion God matches His grace to the response of His people.

It was the beginning of a life based on a new principle. Too often we let problems shut us away from God instead of shutting us in with Him. Jonah was shut up to a miracle, and real faith got its chance. Most of us do not trust the Lord far enough to experience miracles, because faith works best in the context of desperation.

The inside of a fish was not the best place to find oneself, but— bearing in mind what He was about to do—what a provision of God! What a gracious reward to God's servant Jonah after his confession and acceptance of what was to him a death sentence!

"Then Jonah prayed," are the words that begin chapter 2. This was Jonah's immediate reaction; he prayed to the Lord from the belly of the fish. He could have looked upon himself as a piece of flotsam, thrown overboard and left to perish. Would it not seem that God's face was turned away from him? So what was the use of praying?

Yet pray he did, and that was the turning point. Too often we use prayer as a last resort. But if Jonah could pray from the stomach of a fish, after such rebellion and disobedience, then anyone can pray anywhere. His prayer was the token of a broken heart, and the fact that in his extremity his immediate reaction was to seek the Lord was surely evidence that already God had won a great victory in His servant's life.

How wonderful that the sovereign Lord can reach any of us, no matter where we are. Even after Jonah's rebellion and Peter's denial, He was at hand! Many of His people have found this out through experiences very similar to those of Jonah. Listen to the voice of David: "Hear my cry, O God; attend unto my prayer. From the end of the earth will I cry unto thee, when my heart is overwhelmed: Lead me to the rock that is higher than I" (Psalms 61:1, 2).

After the experiences Jonah passed through—well, maybe you and I know just how he felt. In spite of *our* rebellion, we know deep down that the God we worship is the One who comes to the rescue of those of us at the end of our rope. Since Jonah rebelled against the Lord's command to go to Nineveh, there had been no mention of Jonah praying. How true that is! There is no prayer from a rebellious heart, for sin puts a barrier between God and His child.

Let us, therefore, look more closely at this prayer from Jonah's unlikely sanctuary. "I cried by reason of mine affliction unto the Lord, and he heard me; out of the belly of hell cried I, and thou heardest my voice. For *thou* hadst cast me into the deep, . . . all thy billows and thy waves passed over me" (Jonah 2:2, 3, *italics mine*).

Jonah was submitting to the chastisement of God, knowing that all his circumstances had come from the Lord. The storm was raised by God; even the human hands that flung him out of the ship were but instruments in God's hands. Jonah's eyes were opened, even in that dark place, and he was taking his medicine.

How often God's people complain about the situations they find themselves in, resist them, and fail to realize that those circumstances are the whips of God to drive His children to the cross. When we submit to the chastisement of God, we become more patient with others, loving instead of critical, caring instead of hard, our whole attitude reflecting our understanding of the way God has forgiven us.

What strange and contradictory creatures human beings are! Back in chapter 1, Jonah's controlling purpose had been to run away from the presence of the Lord. In chapter 2, he lamented, "Then I said, 'I am cast out from thy presence; how shall I again look upon thy holy temple?' " (Jonah 2:4 RSV).

There is only one reason to fear intimacy with a holy God, and this is because we are living in deliberate and unconfessed sin. But when that sin is acknowledged, once again we may walk in open fellowship with our Lord.

". . . Yet hast thou brought up my life from corruption, O Lord *my* God" (Jonah 2:6, *italics mine*). Jonah's faith was beginning to be reestablished, and suddenly he was aware of that amazing relationship he could still claim; he cried, "O Lord, *my* God!"

We can break our fellowship with the Lord, but we cannot break our relationship. A disobedient child may be out of fellowship with his parents, but he is certainly not out of relationship. Even if he is on the drug scene and cut off from home, yet he is still their child. Even more surely than that, you cannot sever a relationship with God.

God had yet more to do with Jonah. "And the Lord spake unto the fish, and it vomited out Jonah upon the dry land" (Jonah 2:10). It could not take any more prayer warfare! Jonah's prayer of repentance brought resurrection. Once again he experienced liberty; he was free to sacrifice to God with thanksgiving, to pay his vows, and to obey the God he had rejected.

The great lesson here is that at the moment of repentance, the line of communication with heaven is reopened. Therefore restoration to fellowship lies always in our own hands. The Lord waits for our confession, and then He pours out His love and His supply of every spiritual gift and grace.

In modern evangelism, repentance seems to be the forgotten word. It means a change of mind, which leads to a change of behavior. Charles Haddon Spurgeon said, "What is the use of grace which I profess to have received which leaves me exactly the same sort of person as I was before I received it? A faith that does not lead to a drastic change of behavior will never lead to a change of destiny."

Jonah had to be brought down to the depths to learn that lesson, and so have we all. Is your repentance up-to-date? If you are living in a broken relationship with someone, which you have never attempted to repair, then you have never learned what real repentance means. It is far more than remorse: Remorse simply means I am sorry for what sin has done to me. Repentance means I am sorry because of what sin has done to God and to other people. Then I am motivated to change course.

When I meet God at Calvary and change my mind about Him, I know that He is not a God I can keep at a distance, as if He were a kind of policeman. He becomes a God who is infinitely real to me, a sinner, and His face is always turned toward me.

I recognize also the tremendous force of the commandment of Christ, ". . . That ye love one another; as I have loved you . . ." (John 13:34). That means I stand prepared to put right the past, especially where it affects other people, and put it all under the blood of the Cross.

Earlier this century, Dr. F. B. Meyer, one of Britain's great Baptist preachers, was invited to speak at the English Keswick Convention for the first time. He regarded this as a great honor, but he was reluctant to accept because he was having a controversy with the Lord over something he was not prepared to relinquish, even though his ministry was affected and his congregation decreasing.

However, being faced with the challenge of speaking at the convention, Dr. Meyer went up to the Lake District in northwest England, where the little town of Keswick is situated, and climbed one of the mountains. He got down on his knees in prayer and struggled with his problem until at last in utter desperation he cried out, "Lord Jesus, You have had every key to my life except this one! Now please take it from me and have complete control of all there is of me!"

In relating this experience later at the Keswick Convention, Dr. Meyer said, "Do you know what the Lord did? He never took that key, but instead He removed the door! And ever since then, my life has been flooded with 'the light of the knowledge of the glory of God in the face of Jesus Christ' (2 Corinthians 4:6)."

As a result of this testimony, lights in hotels and houses all over Keswick blazed for many hours that night as men and women and young people got right with God. Letters were written, apologies were made, debts were paid—all as the result of the honesty of one man.

Have you got the glory, because in submission to His government, you have been recommissioned by the Lord's grace?

14

Up, Up, and Away!

In 1982, a French expedition tackled the difficult north face of
Mount Everest. During the early part of the climb, a Belgian member of the team fell. After much fruitless searching, he was given up
as dead.

However, he survived the fall and laboriously made his way
down the mountain, finding shelter in a disused monastery in Tibet,
and later reached a village. Finally he got to the capital, Lhasa, but
there he was treated with great suspicion. What would he be doing
there, unless he were a spy? He had no papers to verify his statement, but at last he was allowed to find his way back to Katmandu,
in Nepal.

Imagine the joyous surprise with which he was greeted by the
members of the expedition at the base! Truly he was a man alive
from the dead, a resurrected man!

Jonah had plumbed the depths, but when he was cast on shore,
he became a resurrected man. Why was he spared? What lay ahead
of him?

We are arrested by the startling words in Jonah 3:1 (RSV, *italics
mine*): "*Then* the word of the Lord came to Jonah the second
time. . . ."

In the first chapter we were introduced to four great things that
are tied in with our theme: a great city, a great wind, a great tempest, and a great fish. But all of them fade into insignificance compared with the greatness of the grace of God: "The word of the Lord
came unto Jonah the *second* time." After all Jonah's failure, God
was still prepared to use him.

But that is the way of God! We see it again in His dealing with

Elijah in a cave on Mount Horeb. After a thrilling victory on Mount Carmel, Elijah fled from Jezebel and finally collapsed, exhausted. Then, ". . . The word of the Lord came to him, and he said to him, 'What are you doing here, Elijah?' " (1 Kings 19:9 RSV).

Angry and resentful, Elijah complained, "I am the only true prophet left!" But the Lord spoke to him, not in a wind, or an earthquake, or a fire, but in a still, small voice.

The question was penetrating: "What are you doing here?"

Elijah was concerned with what Ahab and Jezebel were doing; God was concerned with what *he,* Elijah, was doing. Then Elijah wrapped his face in his mantle (which is a good thing to do when tempted to explode), and again the Lord asked the question, ". . . What doest thou here, Elijah?" It was not only a reproof, but a recommissioning.

In the New Testament, we find that the apostle Peter, after he denied his Master, must have thought his days of usefulness and service were over. But in John 21 we read of a meeting with Jesus, who said to him, "Feed my sheep." Peter was not merely forgiven, but sent back to work, like Elijah, Jonah, and many other of the Lord's servants who almost gave up hope.

That is true for us all. What a mercy it is that the Lord does not cast us off! As I look back, I am amazed at God's patience with me, that He has not said, "All right, stand aside!"

Even Paul was afraid of the loss of his service. He wrote, "I pommel my body and subdue it, lest after preaching to others I myself should be disqualified" (1 Corinthians 9:27 RSV). That is a wholesome fear! I do not believe in a second chance after death, but I do believe in a second chance—and, indeed, a million chances—here on earth.

It is never too late to start again. There is no need for the rest of life to be wasted because of one act of disobedience. That is what Satan would have us believe, so that when we are defeated, he can insinuate that everything is totally ruined. "Look what a mess you've made of things! It would be far better for you to quit now before you do more harm!"

But God, in His infinite grace, is able to restore our wasted years, and when lessons have been learned, confession made with genuine repentance, and a strong desire to return to a close walk with Him expressed, He recommissions His servants.

Such is God's grace, but what did that involve for Jonah? "Arise, go unto Nineveh, that great city, and preach unto it the preaching that I bid thee" (Jonah 3:2). What, Nineveh again? Yes, Jonah was told to do what he had refused to do before. The Lord insisted upon obedience to His original orders.

There can be no further light until we obey the light we already have and repent of our disobedience, whatever it may be. It could be something we were afraid to do, a shirking of the discipline of the cross, the battle against sin that we refuse to take up, or love for our enemies that we refuse to show. Whatever it is, our enjoyment of the grace of God requires our submission to His government. Our full salvation demands His full control.

If you want Bible authority for that, here is what Jesus said: "If any man will come after me, let him deny himself, and take up his cross, and follow me. For whosoever will save his life shall lose it: and whosoever will lose his life for my sake shall find it" (Matthew 16:24, 25; *see also* Romans 5:21; 6:16).

The Lord Jesus walked this same path, for it is written of Him that "Though he were a Son, yet learned he obedience by the things which he suffered" (Hebrews 5:8). I have never had the courage to preach from this amazing verse. One thing I know, the Lord never calls His servants to walk along any path that He has not Himself walked.

God tested Jonah's repentance by asking if he was willing to do the thing he had refused to do before. To his eternal credit, Jonah accepted the challenge, having learned the costliness of disobedience. So he started on his way up, back to Nineveh, this time in obedience.

Notice that God's commission was in exactly the same terms as before: "Proclaim the message that I tell you." No preacher has a right to proclaim anything except what he has received from God and what he has been taught in his own walk with the Lord. Paul wrote, "For I received from the Lord what I also delivered to you ..." (1 Corinthians 11:23 RSV). He knew that nothing could get through to his listeners (or readers) unless the Holy Spirit had first driven it home to his own heart.

Recommissioned by God's grace for submission to His divine government, Jonah rose and went to Nineveh (Jonah 3:3). He was right to obey—but do you notice a lack? There was not a word in Jonah's prayer that said anything about his attitude toward Nineveh. I may be wrong, but I do not think the man's heart was in it.

Jonah seemed to obey, not out of love for God, nor any compassion for the lost in Nineveh, but simply out of duty.

On the other hand, we read of the Lord Jesus in John 1:14, "And the Word was made flesh, and dwelt among us, . . . full of grace and truth."

How often we are full of truth but appear to be lacking in grace, and therefore we are very unattractive. Has God spoken to you about being against sin, about loving the unlovely, about sharing His compassion for the lost? But you rebelled and then repented only because of the suffering He put upon you. In spite of all His mercy and the second chance He gave you, your heart is not in it. It is an effort to stick with His call, because the joy has gone.

How long it takes us to learn the depths of our own sinful hearts! Every revelation of God's amazing grace is accompanied by a revelation of our incorrigible sin. Never look for goodness within yourself; for every look at yourself, take ten looks at the risen Lord Jesus. Cease your reluctance and realize the grace given to you as you submit to His government, and then see the amazing results.

Look at Jonah 3:5, "So the people of Nineveh believed God, and they proclaimed a fast, and put on sackcloth, from the greatest of them even to the least of them."

How did it happen so suddenly? Jonah's message itself was forthright, "Yet forty days, and Nineveh shall be overthrown!" It was a very large city, sixty miles in circumference. It took three days to walk through it (*see* Jonah 3:3). Jonah must have felt very insignificant and inadequate, but he had a message from God, and even though he felt sullen, he was true to it.

The Lord Jesus spoke of Jonah in Luke 11:29, 30: "This is an evil generation: they seek a sign; and there shall no sign be given it, but the sign of Jonas the prophet. For as Jonas was a sign unto the Ninevites, so shall also the Son of man be to this generation."

How did Jonah become a sign? Reading between the lines, it would seem obvious that the ship, having thrown out all its cargo, would return to Joppa with the amazing story of the storm and the fate of Jonah. No doubt this story spread along the camel trails to Nineveh, with the information that Jonah originally was supposed to visit that city, until he rebelled.

In that way, perhaps, the Lord prepared the hearts of the people of Nineveh, so that when the prophet appeared, they were ready to listen. And how did he appear? In all probability his physical appearance had been changed dramatically by his sojourn in the stomach of the fish. He might have been an alarming sight, but the Ninevites probably knew that he was a "resurrected" man, alive from a horrible death. While he demonstrated the sign of God's judgment upon disobedience, he revealed also a sign of God's grace.

Every true Christian should be a sign from heaven, not because of what he does or does not do, not because he is able to perform miracles, but because he *is* one! Oh, may we all bear such a stamp of Holy Spirit authority that our life and look and lips speak of heaven! How desperately people like that are needed today, as in past decades God raised up Wesley, Carey, Whitefield, Brainerd, Finney, Spurgeon, Moody, and many others—resurrection men. They all had failed, and sinned, and shirked, but God had spoken to them "a second time," and as they responded, he used them to stir the world.

The record says that "the people of Nineveh believed God." God had spoken to His own people Israel a hundred times, but never with this result. Here one message of authority was given—however reluctantly—and the whole city fell on its knees. Why does that not happen now? Is it because we have too few "resurrection men"? Or is it because we are afraid to face the sacrifice of being such men?

Mark it well: Genuine faith always brings the repentant man on his face before God. In this situation, from the greatest ruler to the least peasant, the Ninevites put on sackcloth.

What a chapter of repentance this is! Jonah repented. Nineveh repented. God repented! "And God saw their works, that they turned from their evil way; and God repented of the evil, that he had said that he would do unto them; and he did it not" (Jonah 3:10).

Does God repent? Yes, He does. His character remains unchangeable: He is always against sin, but He is always ready to bless the sinner who turns from sin to trust in Him. His attitude toward us changes according to our attitude toward Him. Is that not one of the great lessons of this book?

One man's repentance shook Nineveh. Nineveh's repentance moved God to mercy.

This is still true, for 2 Chronicles 7:14 gives us the unchanging commitment the Lord made concerning His people: "If my people, which are called by my name, shall humble themselves, and pray, and seek my face, and turn from their wicked ways; then will I hear from heaven, and will forgive their sin, and will heal their land." Revival is not sparked by a man marching along the street, beating a big drum, but by a repentant soul going back to Calvary with a big sob.

A. W. Tozer wrote, "The whole life of the faithful should be an act of repentance. . . . It must get into every relationship: husband and wife, church, etc. No area of life is unaffected by it. For sin to be forgiven, it must be forsaken. We have learned to live with it."

Jonah had repented of his rebellion; he was up and away, ready to scale the next summit of usefulness to God, but had he reached the final peak? No, he had not yet learned what real repentance was all about.

15

Reduced to Silence

One of the most devastating experiences a climber can have is to find himself backtracking. Instead of going up, he finds himself going down—or going in the wrong direction. He might have been neglectful, momentarily lacking in concentration, or merely careless. He may have ignored his compass, relying upon his sense of direction, which failed him. At such a moment, he urgently needs to stop, to think clearly, and to seek with all his powers to right the wrong. In an experience like that, the climber is reduced to silence, even as Jonah was.

Taking our final glimpse into this book of Jonah, we look again at a man whom God was training and educating to be an obedient disciple. Also, it is the story of God's inner dealing with anyone for whom He has a special purpose. That person must be broken from his self-will and brought to rejection of all that is not God's will. Only then can the Lord use him. Do not be envious of the man whom God uses; stop and reflect upon the discipline he has been put through!

Is there something in your life that is the testing ground of your Christian character and education? To someone it might be an overseas missionary call; to another it might be an issue deep down in his attitude or behavior. The principle to which we must respond is the same—the principle of the cross: our identification with the Lord Jesus and also our willingness to fall into the ground and die (*see* John 12:24).

What vain attempts we often make to claim the substitution without being prepared for the identification! I trust the Holy Spirit will apply Jonah's experience at Nineveh to your own particular circumstances and character.

After all we have seen of the goodness of God in the revival at Nineveh, what would you expect of Jonah? Wouldn't you expect to find Jonah teaching the converts, rejoicing in the blessing, and working to establish and maintain an indigenous church in the city? That is not what happened.

"So Jonah went out of the city, and sat on the east side of the city, and there made him a booth, and sat under it in the shadow, till he might see what would become of the city" (Jonah 4:5). I do not know what he expected to happen to Nineveh, for it had already happened. The city had been deeply shaken and revived from top to bottom.

But Jonah handed in his resignation. God's servant, through whom this great work had been accomplished, sat down under his little shelter and watched the world go by.

Why was Jonah backtracking? "But it displeased Jonah exceedingly, and he was very angry" (Jonah 4:1). God rejoiced! Heaven rejoiced because Nineveh had turned to God. But Jonah was muttering to himself—and to the Lord—"From the very moment God spoke to me about Nineveh, I knew this would happen!

"I knew Him well enough to know that He would want to save these people, if they turned to Him. I knew He was gracious and merciful, abounding in love; He would go to all lengths to save these hateful people. See how they have treated my nation in the past! If God saves our enemies, what will happen to us? Here they are, enjoying all God's blessing in the thrill of revival. God has done the very thing I was afraid He would do, so I am going to resign!"

Isn't it unusual for a preacher to act and talk like that? Not really, for Jonah was not the only prophet who took that attitude. Remember Elijah under the juniper tree?

It was also the attitude of Peter in the city of Joppa, from which Jonah had fled. God sent down a sheet from heaven and told Peter to eat, but Peter saw what he considered to be "unclean" food, and said, "Not so, Lord; for I have never eaten any thing that is common or unclean" (Acts 10:14).

That was also the attitude of the elder brother in the parable of the Prodigal Son, who was so out of harmony with the heart of his father that in anger he cried out, "These many years I have served you, and I never disobeyed your command; yet you never gave me a kid, that I might make merry with my friends. But when this son of yours came, who has devoured your living with harlots, you killed for him the fatted calf!" (Luke 15:29, 30 RSV).

All of us at some time have done the same kind of thing. "I'm the only one who is true to the faith around here! All the others are either modernists or liberals. I stand up for the truth of the Word of God. I will fight to the death to uphold the purity of the faith, and never yield an inch!"

"There is no fellowship around here. No one recognizes what a great vindicator of truth I am, or applauds the stand I take! I think I had better quit!"

So many of us, deep inside perhaps, really have this kind of attitude, which we think is directed toward our fellow Christians, but is really aimed at the Lord. No matter how hard we serve on a committee, or teach a Sunday-school class, or even preach from the pulpit, never have we received a vote of thanks for our labors. So we say, "As long as I am so completely ignored and my work unrecognized, then I resign—perhaps everybody will notice the gap!"

Sadder still is the attitude of the man to whom God speaks concerning some issue in his life, pointing him to Calvary, and in spite of all God's goodness, that man dares to look up into heaven and say, "Not so, Lord."

When there is a controversy I insist upon, when there is an issue before which I will not bend, when there is a cross that I will not accept, when there is a desire for popularity that I will not resist, when I demand that my own virtues should be recognized, when I want my glory and not the Lord's—then there is only one step to "I resign!" Even though I may officially remain in Christian work, in my heart I have handed in my resignation.

Look further in this story of Jonah to find how the Lord dealt with him. The tumult was over—the tempest, the storm, the broken ship, and the great fish. Revival had come to Nineveh, and Jonah's hour in the spotlight was over.

There was one special purpose on God's mind from the first verse to the last of this book, and it was not the salvation of a city but the training of a man—not Nineveh, but Jonah. It was not, in this instance, the decision of an unsaved person that God was after, but the making of a man of God.

The Lord does not merely want people to decide what is right; He desires above all to find someone who will walk with Him, becoming so mature that when he gets to heaven there will not have to be much change. If a man has walked with the Lord through the years, one day, like Enoch, he will find death just a walking home with God into Glory, never to return. If Jonah had not learned his lesson, then it was all in vain.

Perhaps you have found, as I have, that the greatest transactions with the Lord Jesus do not take place in public or in response to an invitation. They take place when you and I are behind closed doors on our knees. Has anything happened there lately? Perhaps your Christian life remains weak because nothing ever happens when you are alone with God.

So the Lord gently took Jonah aside and remonstrated with him. In the opening of the story, the Lord spoke to the prophet with a commission, but He came at last as Friend speaking to friend, as Savior with disciple, as God with His servant. "Then said the Lord, Doest thou well to be angry?" (Jonah 4:4).

God had to teach Jonah a lesson and show him the shallowness of his heart in comparison to all the blessing that had occurred under his ministry.

In chapter 1, God had prepared a great fish, in chapter 4 a gourd vine. "And the Lord God prepared a gourd, and made it to come up over Jonah. . . . So Jonah was exceeding glad of the gourd" (Jonah 4:6). Jonah was a complex character: First he was exceedingly angry, and in verse 6 he was exceedingly glad! He expressed no joy over the revival in the city, but he rejoiced in a little creature comfort.

A strange man, indeed, until we look into our own hearts, for so often we are glad as we bask in the sunshine of something comfortable, while the main issue with God is sidetracked. The tragedy of our old nature is that at one moment we can say yes to identification with the Lord Jesus, and then reject it the next minute. It is not a once-and-for-all business that is settled forever, so that we become a finished product ready for heaven.

Romans 4–8 is not the biography of spiritual growth or of the automatic progress of the Christian. When I accepted the principle of the cross and said no to self and yes to Jesus, I lived in the thrill of Romans 8, but at any moment I am capable of going back to Romans 7 and ending my days in deep carnality. It is not how I begin my life that matters, but how I end it. Reckon yourself dead to sin—and go on reckoning; abide in Christ—and go on abiding.

Head for the summit! Every step you take in disobedience to God has to be followed by a step back again in repentance.

When the Lord allows us for a moment something of comfort, it might prove to be something that sidetracks us from the main issue and causes us to turn aside from the cross. If our Christian work proves tough and hard, we are tempted to seek an easier job without such cost or challenge. When you are sitting comfortably in the shelter of even a little vine, take care, because it might be the means by which the Lord is testing your obedience and discipleship.

"But God prepared a worm when the morning rose the next day, and it smote the gourd that it withered" (Jonah 4:7). Jonah was out in the uncomfortable heat of the sun again.

So it can be with us. If we have rejoiced in temporary comfort, listened to friends who sympathized with our hard-luck stories, and basked in their attention, we may find that it is not a ministry of the Holy Spirit at all. The plant was allowed to come up, and then the worm prepared to destroy it, all in order to teach both Jonah and us a lesson.

Yes, enjoy God's provision of comfort while it is there, but never fail to face the issue with which the Lord is confronting you. If you shirk it, there is real danger that you could end your days outside God's blessing, cut off from the fullness of the joy of the Lord. The coming of the worm teaches us that we can only be happy in the will of God.

". . . When the sun did arise, God prepared a vehement east wind; and the sun beat upon the head of Jonah, that he fainted . . ." (Jonah 4:8). What a plight to be in! The scorching east wind blew from the desert, and no wonder Jonah cried out for the second time, "It is better for me to die than to live." His spirit simply fainted within him, from the glaring sun and the scorching wind. God remonstrated with Jonah in order to point out his sin. But did that have any effect upon that surly servant?

"And God said to Jonah, Doest thou well to be angry for the gourd?" Jonah's defiant reply came, "I do well to be angry, angry even unto death." Jonah was determined not to give in.

But that is not the end of the story. Remember that Jonah wrote this book, putting down God's dealings with him. We would never have known he took that attitude unless he had told us.

In Matthew 12:41, the Lord Jesus said, ". . . a greater than Jonas is here," and the silence of Jonah at the end of his story tells me that the conviction of the Holy Spirit had so overwhelmed Jonah that he was left without a word to say. He wanted to leave this story for all generations to read, not as a picture of Jonah, but as a glorious picture of his God.

Therefore the last word brings us a revelation, for the last word is always with God. Speaking to his angry, red-faced, delinquent servant, the Lord said—and I paraphrase verses 10, 11—"Jonah, do you well to be angry? The plant lasted only a day and a night, and you had nothing to with the making of it or the comfort of it. I did that for you. For a time you were very glad for its shade, but losing it increased your discomfort, and you were sorry and sad.

"Jonah, if you felt like that about a little plant, how much more should I feel compassion for a city that I saw begin more than a thousand years ago? I saw it grow, then its population became mad with sin and drunk with evil. How much more should I have pity upon them? Think of the children in that city—so vulnerable, so defenseless. Should I not have pity on them?"

So the conversation ended, and the controversy was over. Here is one of the greatest revelations in the Old Testament of the character of God, for it anticipates John 3:16, "For God so loved the world, that he gave his only begotten Son. . . ." Yes, God loved the *world,* not just Israel, or a select few, but the whole world. Did Jonah really understand that? Do you and I today, after all the revelation we have in the New Testament, completely understand it?

God prepared Jonah a fish to *save* him, a plant to *shake* him from his resentment, a worm to *shatter* his self-confidence in earthly things, a wind to *silence* him from further controversy with God. May the Lord do these things to us, so that we may focus no more on ourselves, but see Jesus only. Humility is the silence of a soul before God, when there are no more arguments with Him.

May the Lord bring each of us to the place where, knowing that God is right and we are wrong, we are reduced to silence before Him.

16

Debate Ended: Danger Ahead

Would you like to have no more arguments with God? That means total involvement in His plan for your life, which in turn means being ready for anything He may direct. A hundred or more possibilities confront us, but ninety-nine of them are wrong. How to discover the right one—that is the problem!

Luke 11 records the parable of the friend knocking at midnight. I have had problems with this parable—or rather, with what commentators and preachers have said about it. Some have suggested that in this parable the Lord is teaching us to be persistent in prayer. Of course, the whole of the New Testament rings with that necessity. "... Be constant in prayer" (Romans 12:12 RSV). "Continue steadfastly in prayer, being watchful in it with thanksgiving" (Colossians 4:2 RSV). Such is the emphasis of Scripture, but my problem lies in seeing that as the primary thrust of this particular parable.

The usually accepted interpretation is that the man who knocks on the door personifies a believer knocking at heaven's gate in prayer. If he knocks hard enough and long enough and loud enough, eventually God will wake up and do something about him. In order to make that interpretation fit, however, it is necessary to point out an inconsistency: That man in bed was unwilling to respond, but God is always willing.

Obviously this man—so churlish as to refuse to answer because he was snugly in bed, and only eventually rising in order to keep his friend at the door quiet—that could not possibly be God! Unless you admit that, you undermine the whole principle of biblical interpretation.

The truth is, prayer is not overcoming God's reluctance, but rather laying hold of His willingness. In the light of New Testament

127

teaching, I believe the above interpretation of this parable has to be discarded. Surely the principle of all biblical interpretation is a fair treatment of the text in the light of its context and never in contradiction to the complete New Testament revelation.

I found myself, therefore, praying at length and asking the Lord to show me what He meant to say through this parable. He has answered that prayer, so I want to share it with you. I am not surprised to find that several well-esteemed theologians have come to the same conclusion.

Look first at the context: In Luke 11:1 the Lord Jesus was praying, and His disciples must have overheard Him. He could not pray with them because His access to His Father was on a totally different basis. He was without sin, and therefore He had no need to plead a name other than His own; He could go at any moment directly to His Father, whereas everyone else has to plead the merit of sacrifice and cleansing by blood.

As the disciples heard Him pray, they asked, "Lord, teach us to pray." He began by giving them the family prayer (*see* Luke 11:2–4). In that prayer God's name, His glory, and His kingdom come first, but that priority has broken down because of sin. So the prayer goes to the depths of repentance, asking for our Father's forgiveness and for deliverance from temptation. Then the prayer closes in a burst of praise, ". . . For thine is the kingdom, and the power, and the glory, for ever. Amen" (Matthew 6:13).

There are two streams of prayer in the universe. One is the mighty praying of the Lord Jesus, who ever lives and intercedes for us (*see* Hebrews 7:25). The other is a feeble trickle of prayer from each of us which, marvelous to tell, moves the hand that moves the world, if we mean business.

Let me remind you of the prayer of the Lord Jesus in John 17:

> Father. . . . I glorified thee on earth, having accomplished the work which thou gavest me to do. . . . I have manifested thy name to the men whom thou gavest me out of the world. . . . Sanctify them in the truth; thy word is truth. As thou didst send me into the world, so I have sent them into the world. . . . The glory which thou hast given me I have given to them, that they may be one even as we are one. . . . so that the world may know that thou hast sent me. . . .
>
> John 17:1, 4, 6, 17, 18, 22, 23 RSV

Jesus prayed that you and I might believe in the amazing miracle: God in humanity, displaying to the world the reality of God's love in people who have received the Word and therefore know the glory, so that others will see and believe because of them. If ever there was a time in the history of the Church when we need the Word and the glory, it is today. Not one without the other, but both together. The Word of God and the glory of the Spirit in our hearts enable us to witness to Him effectively. It is for this that Jesus was praying.

But that prayer does not seem to be receiving much in the way of an answer, because the Church goes on halfheartedly, with no apparent desire to be all it might be. So many Christians go on doing their "thing," seeming not to want the glory (afraid of it, maybe?), and just carrying on with the program.

Now and again people begin to see the emptiness of "playing church" and that Christian faith apart from the glory is a losing game. The tragedy of the church is that its glory has faded; therefore the society in which we live is gaining in depravity and evil as the church retreats behind closed doors. But the Lord has His people who want the glory and the Word and are prepared for Him to use them. A little trickle of prayer from a few here and there who mean business—and God answers!

Who, then, was this suppliant at midnight? "Which of you shall have a friend, and shall go unto him at midnight, and say unto him, Friend, lend me three loaves . . ." (Luke 11:5). In Mark 13:35, Jesus said to His disciples, "Watch ye therefore: for ye know not when the master of the house cometh, at even, or at midnight. . . ." Again, in the parable of the ten virgins in Matthew 25:1–13, as they all slept, "At midnight there was a cry made, Behold, the bridegroom cometh. . . ."

Who was this suppliant at midnight? Surely it would be the Lord Jesus Himself. Midnight—the hour of His return. Here is, I believe, a graphic picture of the Lord knocking at the door.

"But," you may ask, "at what door?"

The door of the impenitent heart? But there comes a time when He stops knocking at that door. If you want to go your own way and insist on doing your own thing, His Spirit will not interfere with your free will, but you must bear the consequences.

This, however, was a *friend* who knocked at the door, and it was a *friend* who was inside. At Laodicea, it was on a church door that the risen Lord knocked at the midnight hour. To that church, which professed to be rich, increased with goods, contented, and in need of nothing, Jesus said, ". . . Thou art wretched, and miserable, and poor, and blind, and naked" (Revelation 3:17). In other words, "You think you have so much, but you are spiritually poor! And I, your Risen Lord, knock at the door, asking to come in and meet your real needs."

In the world's history it approaches midnight, and yet we see the church rich, contented, programmed, equipped—and Jesus waits outside. It has been years since anything in the way of a miracle happened in the average church.

I am reminded of that lovely story in Mark 10:46–52. Jesus was having important discussions with the Pharisees. Then He presented a new revelation of His program to His disciples, telling them that His face was steadfastly set toward Jerusalem.

But listen! ". . . Jesus, thou son of David, have mercy on me," cried out a man by the side of the road. All Jesus' discussions with the Pharisees, all His revelations to His disciples, all His determined steps toward Jerusalem, were stopped for a moment, because one poor beggar was calling Him.

My friend, if that does not reach you, what will? We load our churches with committees and have no time for what Christianity is all about, which is one-on-one contact for Christ. Poor Bartimaeus, in his desperate need, would not have much chance of being heard today. We are too busy raising funds for new buildings, to go out and share Jesus with those who need Him.

Back now to our parable in Luke 11. There was another, behind-the-scenes character. The man knocking at the door said, "A friend of mine in his journey is come to me, and I have nothing to set before him" (Luke 11:6). Who could this be? Surely it was a person with no knowledge of God and without hope, for the One who knocked said, "I have nothing to set before him."

There is a cry going up to the Lord today from all over the earth. It is not articulate, because miserable, lost humanity cannot fathom what has gone wrong. They are groping in the dark, but their cry is going up to God. He hears them and calls to His Church, "Friend, lend *Me* three loaves, for there is a friend of Mine on his journey, lost, and I have nothing to put before him."

"Wait a minute," you say to me. "That cannot possibly be God, for He can do anything."

Yes, God *can* do anything, but in His sovereignty He does it through human instruments.

Let me ask you three questions:

First, does the sacrifice of Jesus on the cross provide adequate salvation for everybody from creation until now? Yes, Hebrews 10:10 (RSV) says, "We have been sanctified through the offering of the body of Jesus Christ once for all."

Second, does that mean that everyone will be saved because Jesus died on the cross? I would like to be able to say yes, but that is against the teaching of Scriptures such as John 3:16 (*italics mine*), ". . . that *whosoever believeth* in him should not perish, but have everlasting life." The sacrifice of Jesus Christ is adequate for the salvation of all, but it is effective only in the lives of those who believe and repent.

Third, can anyone be saved without hearing? The answer is stated clearly in Romans 10:13–15: "For whosoever shall call upon the name of the Lord shall be saved. How then shall they call on him in whom they have not believed? and how shall they believe in him of whom they have not heard? and how shall they hear without a preacher? And how shall they preach except they be sent? . . ."

This makes it perfectly clear that those who come to know the Lord Jesus have been led to Him by the sovereign grace of God, but always through some human instrumentality. This is fully seen in the parable we are studying.

The risen Lord Jesus, on the very verge of His return at midnight, pleads at the door of His church, "Friend, here is another friend. You don't see him, but I do, and his cry has come up to Me. But I have nothing to put before him—I have no doctor, no nurse, no teacher, no one who cares, no messenger—and people are *lost* in the journey of life."

In Scotland, a television program was depicting some of the tragedies of drug addiction, and teenagers were being interviewed on the subject. A girl was sitting before the interviewer, who said to her, "How old are you?"

"Seventeen," she replied.

"Are you on drugs?"

"Yes," was her terse answer.

"What are you taking?"

"Heroin," came the same toneless voice.

Looking her straight in the face, the man asked, "Aren't you afraid it will kill you?"

That girl turned in her chair, looked right at the camera—right into my eyes and the eyes of all who were watching—and with a look of blank despair she said, "I hope to God it will, and that quickly."

See the average fundamental church, "rich, increased with goods, and in need of nothing," with its streamlined program. A girl like that can never be reached through a program—never! It is my conviction that this generation of Christians will stand at the judgment seat of Christ to be judged for our refusal to get involved. Multitudes are going to hell, knowing nothing of Jesus and His mighty act of redemption or the Holy Spirit with His life-changing power. The current of redemptive love is stagnating in us. We are too sleepy to care, like Peter and the others in Gethsemane. The thing Christ dreaded was that when He comes He should find His people asleep: "Watch ye therefore. . . . lest coming suddenly he find you sleeping" (Mark 13:35, 36).

Listen to the request of Jesus, "Friend, lend *Me* three loaves. . . ."

Then see the speed of God's answer to a soul that responds, "Ask, and it shall be given you; seek, and ye shall find; knock, and it shall be opened unto you. . . . If ye then, being evil, know how to give good gifts unto your children, how much more shall your heavenly Father give the Holy Spirit to them that ask Him?" (Luke 11:9, 13).

Is that not the whole story of the Bible? God is eager to meet us and to forgive us. At the first longing on the part of a child of God that his life should be utterly used in Christ's service, God gives enablement by His Holy Spirit.

At the midnight hour in the world's history, Jesus knocks at the door of your life and mine, and He speaks about a friend of His who is lost in the journey of life. "Friend, lend Me *your life*. Lend Me your skills, your education, your career."

"Oh, Lord, I can't! I know I should, but I'm afraid. I'll work harder, double my tithe, give more to missions—"

"No," says the Lord, "Give Me your *life*." Will you put your life at risk? A Christian knows that ultimately he is secure, but in the immediate present life may get turned upside down. When you lend the Lord your life, you begin to live dangerously.

I believe it was Dr. Paul Rees, the former beloved president of World Vision, who said in my hearing that there is danger in caring. If you don't care, you become hard. But if you become vulnerable to other people's hurts, that is costly. Put a shell around you, settle down in your me-first life-style, and you save yourself a lot of pain. But live for Jesus, and it may disturb your home, your program, everything.

Then there is danger in daring. Our church committees, most of them so conventional and computerized, need to get down on their knees and ask for a spiritual shock treatment. If given half a chance, the Holy Spirit would send through us a galvanizing wave of vitality to rescue us from our velvet ruts. We are afraid to break into some new adventure for the Lord, for our slogan is—and has been for years—"Habit, be my friend!" But Jesus says, "No! *Danger* be your friend!"

Also, there is danger in sharing, because when you really share the love of Jesus with someone, you do not notice his color or race; you do not worry about his background; and that can be uncomfortable. Nor do you ask that wounded person how he is feeling, for you yourself feel his pain as you share.

There is only One who can do that completely, Jesus Himself, and He is calling today. It may be our last chance. He is calling to lift us out of our beds, saying, "Friend, lend Me your life."

It has been my privilege to visit many overseas mission fields, and I have found men and women there who have taken early retirement from business and gone out to serve the Lord as radio engineers, technicians, motor mechanics, builders, accountants, doctors—you name it! They are filling vital positions, and many a station could never be kept open but for people like that, often older people who left comfortable homes and the delights of retirement, all for Jesus' sake.

When visiting what was once called the Congo, I met a lady who was translating the Bible into the language of the people. I asked her how old she was, and she said she was seventy-four.

"When are you taking your next furlough?" I asked.

Looking at me with a twinkle in her eye, she said, "In heaven!"

Friend, lend Jesus *your* life. Do you believe the Lord is saying that to you? Are you prepared to forget your comfort and lend the Lord however many or few years that are left? Each one has to answer the Lord who asks for our total commitment. When you respond, you will find that the Lord provides all your need: "How *much more* will the heavenly Father give the Holy Spirit to those who ask Him?" The enduement of the Holy Spirit gives us the power to be useful in service for the Lord.

17

Wanted: A Man

There are times when a mountaineer is within sight of the summit, yet the stiffest part of the climb lies ahead. He pauses, looks back on the view, and surveys the threatening massif before him. He takes stock and wonders if he has sufficient oxygen to make it at such a high altitude. Many have died on high climbs, because they underestimated this vital necessity.

Prayer is the Christian's vital breath, the oxygen of the soul. As we have seen, the enduement of the Holy Spirit comes upon those who cease their arguments with God and accept the responsibility of living in a close and vital relationship with Him in the place of His choosing. Nevertheless, the Christian mountaineer must look to his supply of oxygen constantly, because without prayer he withers and dies. Without it he becomes spiritually ineffective.

There are two amazing passages in the Old Testament on which I wish to base this study. The first is in Ezekiel 22:30. "And I sought for a man among them, that should make up the hedge, and stand in the gap before me for the land, that I should not destroy it: but I found none." The second is Isaiah 59:16 (RSV), which reads, "He saw that there was no man, and wondered that there was no one to intervene; then his own arm brought him victory, and his righteousness upheld him."

We hear of people searching for God, and men need to seek Him. The Lord Jesus Himself bids us to ask, seek, and knock. The message through Jeremiah is, "And ye shall seek me, and find me, when ye shall search for me with all your heart. And I will be found of you, saith the Lord . . ." (Jeremiah 29:13, 14).

In the two passages quoted, this is reversed: The Lord is seeking for a man. He is always doing that; He does not seek a group of

135

people—not for a drama group, or a singing group, or any other group of which there are scores around—but He wants a *man*. How entertainment has taken over! Many in these groups are truly dedicated to the Lord and used by Him, but it is through the preaching of the cross that men are saved.

In the letters to the New Testament churches (Revelation 2, 3), repeatedly it is written, "He who has an ear, let him hear what the Spirit saith to the churches" (2:7, 11, 17, and so on). God looks for just one man who will listen and take time to hear what He wants to say. In the feverish activity of so many churches today—often with a very good object—He has little chance to be heard. "And he wondered that there was no intercessor."

The question is constantly asked, How can we possibly intervene in society? There is no way in which Christians can make an effective impact upon world situations—except one, and that is through prayer, which gives us access to the highest throne in the universe. It is encouraging to recall the words of 2 Chronicles 7:14, "If my people, which are called by my name, shall humble themselves, and pray, ... then will I hear from heaven, and will forgive their sin, and will heal their land."

It is very significant today, when every country is in such straits and the world is in such turmoil, that there are those to whom the Lord has spoken through that verse and who are now being used as intercessors. I think particularly of the Lydia Fellowship for ladies, the impact of Evelyn Christiansen, the interfaith meetings for prayer in Northern Ireland, and the vision of George Verwer of Operation Mobilization.

I recall that when I was a pastor at Moody Memorial Church in Chicago, George was a student at Moody Bible Institute. He would visit me about once a month for prayer and counsel, and when we had a series of half-nights of prayer, he was present. Now if you go to any Operation Mobilization Conference, a night or half-night of prayer is always on the agenda, because George recognized the importance of intercession.

So far as churches are concerned, there is the Young Nak Church, in Seoul, Korea. When my wife and I visited that country, we were awakened by bells ringing out a hymn tune at 5:30 A.M.— the church calling the people to prayer. That happens every day, and has been going on for years. But it is an exception.

In the National Gallery in London hangs a painting of General

William Booth, founder of the Salvation Army. He is portrayed sitting at his desk before an open Bible, in an attitude of prayer. One day when the curator was closing the gallery, he heard a voice from one of the rooms. He found a man on his knees before this portrait, sobbing, "Do it again, Lord! Do it again!" Do we know prayer and concern like that? Has our oxygen supply run low or ceased altogether?

Consider the priority of prayer. Most Christians who are honest would acknowledge that this is the weakest area in their personal life and possibly in their church life. A well-known Christian leader said, "When I go to prayer, I find my heart so loth to go to God; and when it is with Him, so loth to stay."

We always contrive to find time for whatever we think most important. Too often, we curtail time spent in prayer. It is said that Martin Luther, when asked about his plans for the next day, replied, "It is work from early till late; in fact, I have so much to do I will spend the first three hours in prayer."

If prayer could have been dispensed with in any life, surely it would have been in that of the sinless Son of Man. Yet it was a dominating feature of His life. He often rose a great while before day in order to have unbroken communion with His Father (*see* Mark 1:35). Luke 6:12 says, ". . . He went out into a mountain to pray, and continued all night in prayer to God."

Then in Luke 5:16 we are told, "And he withdrew himself into the wilderness, and prayed." This would appear to have been a regular habit, and by word and example He impressed upon His disciples the importance of solitude in prayer (*see* Mark 6:46).

To all of us, the example of the Lord in His prayer life is a great challenge. Both Christ and Paul made it clear that true prayer is not just a dreamy reverie. "All intercession is a sacrifice, a bleeding sacrifice," said J. H. Jowett. Jesus performed many mighty works without outward sign of strain, but of His praying it is recorded that He ". . . offered up prayers and supplications with strong crying and tears . . ." (Hebrews 5:7).

If prayer was a priority in the life of the Lord Jesus, how much more so for you and me! Let us see that the oxygen container is constantly replenished on our climb to the summit!

Prayer also has a price, because sometimes we are tempted to wonder if anything happens at the other end of the line. In Isaiah 58, the people were complaining that in spite of continual fasting, they were not enjoying the blessings of God. His answer was that they were going about it in the wrong way (58:3, 4). God turned the whole responsibility back upon them. If they accused Him of inactivity, He pointed to their sin (59:2, 3). *They* shut their eyes to His law, and He shut *His* eyes to their deliverance.

Could not the language of Isaish 59:9–11 be applied to our world today, especially in every country overrun by the communist bloc? Why is God apparently inactive, and everything seems to proceed as though He were dead? That is not only true nationally, but personally. A wrong relationship with God, no matter what else may be right in our lives, inevitably blocks His purpose from being fulfilled. We need to remember that the supply of His grace is never in conflict with the demands of His holiness.

The Lord said He is not deaf, but if we want Him to hear us, we have to break down the barrier which comes between Him and us—from our side. Sin must be forsaken (Isaiah 59:1, 2). But instead of doing that, Israel had forsaken prayer. No wonder the Lord was amazed that there was no man bold enough to face the tide of corruption and declare the way of truth. Nor was there one who would give himself to prayer to turn away the wrath of God.

The price involved is great: "Brethren, my heart's desire and *prayer* to God for Israel is, that they might be saved" (Romans 10:1, *italics mine*). "My prayer" is very different from "my praying."

In *East Asia Millions,* A. J. Mathews defines the difference.

> Uninvolved Christianity has little inclination for the sacrifice of time and convenience demanded. Consequently the church has lost its attack-power—and this at a time when the devil is deploying his forces for a grand assault. But for those willing to commit themselves to Christ for this kind of warfare, enlistment could well be the watershed of their lives. . . . We learn how few things are really essential, but how essential these few things really are. One of these is *my prayer.*

In Romans 8:26, 27 Paul describes real prayer: "Likewise the Spirit also helpeth our infirmities: for we know not what we should pray for as we ought: but the Spirit itself maketh intercession for us with groanings which cannot be uttered. And he that searcheth the hearts knoweth what is the mind of the Spirit, because he maketh intercession for the saints according to the will of God."

My *praying* is just the words I say at the prayer meeting, when I know what will be acceptable, but it rarely reveals my true thoughts or the deep needs of my heart. That is all too personal, and maybe no one would understand. But "my prayer" is the cry of my heart, which is too deep for words, and a relying upon the Holy Spirit to intercede for me. This is the true oxygen of the soul!

Now let us think of the power of prayer, for this is the area in which most of us are weakest. A specious theological argument is made on the fact that Jesus said, "... For your heavenly Father knoweth that ye have need of all these things" (Matthew 6:32). So why bother to pray?

If God is sovereign and all things are under His control, why should we pray at all? That viewpoint would excuse us from all participation. But Paul said, "My little children, with whom I am again *in travail* until Christ be formed in you!" (Galatians 4:19 RSV, *italics mine*). In Ephesians 3:14–21, Paul also prefaced a magnificent prayer by saying, "For this cause I bow my knees unto the Father. . . ." Paul knew the priority, and the price, as well as the power of prayer.

Over and over again the New Testament emphasizes the priority of prayer. When we come to Jesus at Calvary, to claim Him as Lord and Savior, we think of the cross as something we come into to get through. The truth is, we come into it to be identified with it, and that is the whole purpose of prayer. We do not pray in order to receive answers, but to be identified with the will of God for our lives.

The devil's great concern is to keep us from prayer. He loves to see us up to the eyes in work, provided we don't pray. He does not fear our eager Bible study, provided we don't pray. He laughs at our toiling and mocks at our wisdom, but trembles when we pray.

Dr. A. J. Gordon said, "You can do more than pray when you have prayed; but you can never do more than pray until you have prayed." If only we believed that! That is why God wonders not merely that nobody is there to intercede, but also that there is no one humble enough to approach Him on the only basis that can make such intercession possible, casting ourselves utterly on the mercy of God.

The trouble is that when we pray, we act like the people in

Isaiah's time and fail to face our own spiritual poverty. "He will regard the prayer of the destitute, and not despise their prayer" (Psalms 102:17). It is a deadful thing to be destitute—homeless, friendless, penniless, at the end of our rope. But one of the curses of twentieth-century Christianity is that we are *not* destitute. We are utterly self-sufficient, yet our sufficiency, help, and hope should be, not in a church program or in a university degree, but in *God.*

Let us face this squarely and ask God to keep us in the place where He shows His power, because only there do we really acknowledge we are destitute. Otherwise we miss the miracle.

In the economic and political world, we see spiraling inflation, massive unemployment, and all the other problems of overpopulation and overproduction. These ills are also accelerated by individual and national status seeking. Everyone trying to get one rung higher on the ladder than the next man causes a mad scramble for power. The favorite motto is, "You first—after me!"

How different should be the attitude of the believer. We are warned by Paul not to be conformed to this world, but to be transformed. The translation by J. B. Phillips put it: "Don't let the world around you squeeze you into its own mould" (Romans 12:2). When we stand before the cross, the ground is level, and we all meet as brothers and sisters who are destitute apart from the grace of God. We have no claim to His love, except by His grace and mercy.

That is always the correct approach to God, not only for a sinner, but also for a saint. If we are too big to come to Him that way, we can never touch His throne. We must come in a spirit of helplessness to cast ourselves utterly on His mercy.

How many times David cried out, "O Lord!" And he wrote, "As the hart panteth after the water brooks, so panteth my soul after thee, O God" (Psalms 42:1). Hannah, in bitterness of spirit, prayed to the Lord and wept as she began her vow, ". . . O Lord of hosts . . ." (1 Samuel 1:10, 11). The "O" has gone out of our praying, therefore we have little effective prayer. We seldom cry the "O Lord!" of desperation.

The Reverend David Watson said, "What do you do when what you have been taught to believe no longer rings a bell in your experience? Either you change your theology to fit your experience and say, 'God is dead' because your experience of Him is dead, or you will keep hold firmly on Bible truth, and thirst for the living God."

It was said of John Wesley that he possessed the unusual combination of a cool head and a warm heart. To have only a cool head means that person will play things safe, hold open-ended discussions, and in fact do anything except get filled with the Holy Spirit and go out where the action is, telling people about the Lord Jesus.

There is power in prayer, like the life-giving oxygen that fills the lungs with every breath we take. There are also many promises that are ours in answer to prayer. In spite of our failure to man this strategic battlefront, God's purposes may be delayed, but they cannot be thwarted. Ultimately He will have the victory, and then if we really pray, the promise of Isaiah 59:19 becomes true,". . . When the enemy shall come in like a flood, the Spirit of the Lord shall lift up a standard against him."

The highest positions in the kingdom are reserved for those who have qualified in secret. Your name may never be heard of on earth, but it will be well-known in heaven. Christian leadership is attained not by publicity, but by obscurity. *This* is the power of prayer so few of us know anything about.

Who will face the challenge of being an intercessor? It may mean examining your calendar and eliminating unnecessary engagements in order to allow time for this vital ministry. It may call for reestablishing family worship and prayer, putting the Lord back into the central place in your home. Whatever it is, are you prepared to do it? Only then can you look up into the Lord's face and say, "Lord, here am I!"

18

Climbing on Track

During my first pastorate, we lived in Richmond, near London. Every Sunday morning for a time, while we were preparing to go to the morning service, we would hear the unmistakable sound of the first passenger jet plane, the Comet, coming over our house on its way to London Airport. One Sunday in 1953 we missed it. Had we grown so used to it that we did not notice? No, the next day in the papers we read the appalling news that it had crashed outside Calcutta, killing passengers and crew.

On that plane was Mr. Fred Mitchell, chairman of the English Keswick Convention and general director of the China Inland Mission, as it was called at that time. He was on his way home from Singapore, via Calcutta, when the plane crashed. The final word from the pilot to the Calcutta control tower was "Climbing on track." That is the title Miss Phyllis Thompson gave to the biography she wrote of Mr. Mitchell. It summarized his life perfectly, for he closely followed his Lord and grew like Him in character. Although his body crashed to the ground, in spirit he was still climbing until he saw his Savior's face.

This is also true as we head for the summit, for as Leonard Ravenhill has said, "There are no short cuts to the high peaks of spirituality, and no ski-lifts." Worldwide, the faith of Christian people is being tested today, and the climb is steep.

Many lessons can be learned about this principle of climbing, particularly in relation to the subject of faith. How much our Lord had to say about this! Let us look at one specific incident recorded in Matthew 15:21–31. It occurred at a significant moment in the ministry of the Lord Jesus. It had become obvious that He was not being accepted as the Messiah, and He sought rest and solitude by departing into the region of Tyre and Sidon. That departure marked a definite crisis: It brought the Jews' rejection of Himself clearly in view.

At the same time, it introduced the first Gentile convert. She was a Canaanite woman (Matthew 15:22), whom Mark further identified as "a Greek, a Syrophenician by nation . . ." (Mark 7:26). She was therefore a direct descendant of outcasts, people who had been swept away in the divine economy of the past because of their sin, in order for God to make way for His people Israel. She was outside the covenant of Israel, a worshiper of pagan gods. Yet from such Jesus ". . . could not be hid" (*see* Mark 7:24).

If He so desired, He could hide Himself. We read in John 8:59, ". . . Jesus hid himself, and went out of the temple. . . ." From intellectual pride and orthodox tradition and prejudice, He always hides Himself.

Jesus never dealt with two people in the same way. His approach was always different, which reveals to us the infinite variety of human need and His inexhaustible capacity to meet it all. This can be an example for all of us, because it is so easy to pigeonhole people and bring out our proof texts without really listening to their problems.

Yet our approach to Jesus, if it is to establish vital contact, must always be on the same principle of faith and trust. Look at the triumph of this woman's faith against every discouragement. Her faith clung to the Lord in desperation, recognizing that there was no hope anywhere else. None but He could save her child so ". . . grievously vexed with a devil" (Matthew 15:22).

It is a record of faith overcoming obstacles that the Lord Himself seemed to put in her way. Yet she held on until her need was met. Faith works best in the context of desperation. You can prove the truth of this by asking yourself the question, "Just how much and how far am *I* prepared to trust the Lord?"

Sometimes we are perplexed and bewildered by the Lord's dealings with us. It is a good thing to look at the outcome of a testing, for only then can we understand the process. That will be supremely true when we arrive in heaven, for then we shall know and understand, as we cannot possibly understand now.

Meanwhile, let us look at the Lord's way with this woman whose daughter was possessed by a demon; then perhaps we shall begin to appreciate more clearly His way with us. Four times in Matthew's account we read that He answered her cry.

"But he answered her not a word . . ." (Matthew 15:23). This was the answer of denial.

Then He answered, "I am not sent but unto the lost sheep of the house of Israel." This was the answer of discouragement.

Again He answered, "It is not meet to take the children's bread, and to cast it to dogs." This was the answer of disillusionment.

At last Jesus answered her, "O woman, great is thy faith . . ." (Matthew 15:28). This was the answer of deliverance.

Here the Lord Jesus found living faith in a most unlikely place, in surroundings from which orthodoxy had withdrawn in condemnation. How empty is knowledge without faith! You and I are not saved by *what* we believe, but by the One on whom we believe. Never forget that! Where there is little knowledge and encouragement, and where the soil is barren, the Lord is still able to find strong faith. The choicest of Christians can live in apparently impossible surroundings. Our heavenly Father has children everywhere, and He enables them all to grow, provided their roots are deeply embedded in Himself, drawing upon the life of the indwelling Holy Spirit. And the Lord trains us all so that we share a family likeness and learn to mature. We should not be surprised if He tests how we react under conditions of stress.

Three times Jesus put this woman's trust in Him to a fierce test; in fact, in Matthew 15:23, 24 He seemed to reject her. Three times she appealed to His love, and finally her request was granted. Her faith was immediately rewarded, and she gained a lifelong blessing that was capable of withstanding any number of stresses. A faith not worth testing is not worth having. If on the climb we turn back at the first obstacle, our steadfastness of purpose would be seriously under question.

Now look at the interview in detail: "And, behold, a woman of Canaan came out of the same coasts and cried unto him, saying, Have mercy on me, O Lord, thou son of David; my daughter is grievously vexed with a devil. But he answered her not a word . . ." (Matthew 15:22, 23). To think of Christ being silent to a cry like that seems to contradict the whole Gospel story! She had thrown herself at His feet, for her heart was broken, yet He appeared to ignore her. But was that silence a denial? How often we have assumed so and given up praying. When there is no sign of an answer, day after day, and even year after year, prayer seems to us to be a failure.

But look more closely: How had she come to Christ? She said, "Son of David," and appealed to Him as the Messiah of the Jews. As a Gentile, she had no claim on Him in that capacity; was that why He remained silent? This much I do know, that silence is not denial. It is often His way of discipline and testing, and it can be that we too have come to God on the wrong basis. There is only one ground of approach to the Throne of heaven, and that is through Christ's atoning death on the cross. The writer to the Hebrews makes this very clear:

> Having therefore, brethren, boldness to enter into the holiest by the blood of Jesus, By a new and living way, which he hath consecrated for us, through the veil, that is to say, his flesh; And having an high priest over the house of God; Let us draw near with a true heart in full assurance of faith, having our hearts sprinkled from an evil conscience, and our bodies washed with pure water.
>
> Hebrews 10:19–22

That is the only way for anyone to come to Him. Make sure that His silence to your prayer is not because you keep coming on some other ground. He may be testing you, but He will never *deny* you unless you try to come some other way. It is through faith in the Lord Jesus Christ alone that we have access to God's grace. May we never be too big to come that way, for if we try it, we are not on "praying ground," and He cannot answer us.

There came a strange response from the disciples listening in— and it comes uncomfortably close to each one of us. ". . . Send her away," they advised the Lord, "for she crieth after us" (Matthew 15:23). To them she was only a nuisance; they all thought her very presumptuous. "She is crying after *us!*" they said—what presumption on their part!

What a lesson for us! There are many disciples today who begin to presume that people are coming to hear *them,* to follow *them,* when it is the Lord Jesus the people desperately need. People are often repelled by cold words, unkind behavior, or unsympathetic treatment from the Lord's disciples. But this woman did not let that keep her from pressing her claim upon Christ.

Please follow her example, and don't let any treatment you may receive at the hands of Christians keep you away from the Lord Jesus. Keep pressing on to get into His presence, even though His answer may seem discouraging. When He said, "I am not sent but unto the lost sheep of the house of Israel," it seemed to cut her off from all hope. She was not of the house of Israel. No, but she was one of His lost sheep, for He said in John 10:16 (RSV), "I have other sheep, that are not of this fold; I must bring them also, and they will heed my voice." Sensing this, she clung to Him and cried, "Lord, help me!"

To some people, the doctrine of divine choice, which is plainly taught in the Scriptures, can have a discouraging effect. They go through life wondering whether or not they are predestined for eternal life. But remember that our election is *in Christ*. There is not one person who has ever come to God on the ground of Calvary and been turned away.

Now read the Lord's third answer: "It is not meet to take the children's bread, and cast it to the dogs."

"Truth, Lord," she said, "yet the dogs eat of the crumbs which fall from their masters' table" (Matthew 15:26, 27).

That answer would seem almost worse than silence! To the Jew, the Gentile was but a dog. This woman was not only outside any covenant relationship with Christ, but she was utterly unworthy in herself to receive anything from Him.

Yet she did not dispute the fact and said to Him, in effect, "Truly, Lord, I have no merit and no right to come, only my desperate need. It would not be fitting for one of Your children to be deprived of anything for me. Though I am but a dog, You are my Lord for all that." Not only did she not dispute with Him, but she worshiped the hand that chastened so sorely and bowed reverently before the One who spoke so sternly.

My friend, even though you feel as unworthy as she, and you are disillusioned concerning any goodness in yourself, please remember that your salvation does not rest upon anything that you are or ever can be. Jesus does not bless someone because of how good he is, but because he comes to Him as a beggar. You need to be saved *from* yourself, not *by* yourself.

God's plan is for you to be emptied that He may fill you, to confess your sinfulness that He may wash you, to be nothing that He may be everything to you. Never allow the frequency or blackness of your sin to keep you from believing prayer. Faith accepts the verdict of God's Word upon the old nature, that in you is nothing inherently good. If that word comes as balm to the wound, or as a sword to slay, don't fight against it. You can never find God by refusing to admit the truth of what He says. In yielding alone lies the path of safety.

This woman pressed home her claim by argument. She saw a gleam of hope! There are two words for *dog* in Scripture. One speaks of the scavenger dog of the street, the pariah; the other is the little dog of the household, which sits at the feet of the children by the table and eats the crumbs, and *this* is the word Jesus used.

So the woman flung herself upon His mercy and began to argue on the basis of this one word. She accepted His statement, as if to say, "I'm only a little dog, but because of that I have claim to a crumb. Lord, that is all I want! Not the children's bread, but only a crumb, the share of the dog under the table!"

Now you see how she reacted to the answer of disillusionment, and you can adopt that attitude, too. "I agree with the Lord's verdict that there is no good in myself. But Lord, I am under the sound of the Gospel, so if I am a hearer of the truth, surely I can be a receiver, too! I am Your property by creation. There is enough in Your overflowing mercy for all Your children, and if you bless me, You are none the poorer. You are just as rich in power to forgive and cleanse as ever!"

It has always been the Lord's purpose that, through the children, the "dogs" should get the bread of life. In other words, His plan has been to reach the lost through those He has already saved.

Finally, read Christ's answer of deliverance in Matthew 15:28, "O woman, great is thy faith: be it unto thee even as thou wilt. . . ." And her daughter was healed instantly. It was as if the Lord of Glory surrendered to the conquering power of her great faith. After He had tried and tested her, and in proving her found a faith like pure gold, she gained her desire.

What a comfort to those who think there is no hope for them. Press your claim upon His mercy. Maybe you have prayed, but have given up, and you have even tried to reform and make yourself better, but have failed miserably. Of course you have! Cling to the cross, even if the world seems to shatter around you. For if you really hold on to the Lord Jesus, you can never perish there.

What a challenge we find here concerning our praying for others!

The woman asked for the sake of her daughter. Do we pray, as she did, on behalf of our own children, or grandchildren, or young people in general?

What a lesson there is here on the effect one's faith can have in blessing others. In Matthew 15:29–31 we read of Jesus departing through the Gentile areas, and as the crowds came to Him, bringing all their sick folk, He healed them. The same grace for which the woman had pleaded so hard seemed to flow unasked. She wrung out a crumb. Now the crowds had whole loaves with little asking. Did her faith create faith in others? Had it proved to be infectious?

Jesus has no difficulties in the presence of faith, for when people come to Him with a great burden and cast it at His feet, they experience His delivering power. If they come His appointed way, accepting His verdict upon their unworthiness and pressing home their claim upon His mercy, they find it true that ". . . him that cometh to me I will in no wise cast out" (John 6:37).

Are you climbing on track, growing in faith and knowledge of the Lord Jesus, through intimate communion with Him?

19

The Greatness of Forgiveness

The subject of forgiveness is not easy either to write about or to read. It is demanding, the sort of theme that cannot be skirted around, but I must admit it is not often I have spoken on forgiveness in just this way.

The basis for our study is Matthew 18:21–35, but it is worth reading the whole chapter in order to get the complete context. It opens with the Lord Jesus rebuking His status-seeking disciples by giving them a lesson on the simplicity of a child—not being childish, but childlike, submissive, and obedient.

Then He goes on to give a stern warning to those who offend and cause others to stumble (Matthew 18:5, 6). It would be better for such a person to have his life cut short rather than to cause a young believer to fall into sin. How often this happens when someone from a non-Christian home becomes a believer in the Lord Jesus and the rest of the family scoffs and sneers, trying every way to turn him or her from the faith. Such an attitude will merit a stern rebuke from the Lord of Glory.

In verses 7–9 the Lord speaks of the way He would have us deal with that part of us which offends others. These are strong words, and it must be remembered that they came from the lips of the One who was love incarnate.

But what about those who do offend? Is there no forgiveness? So we come to the second part of the chapter, and if the teaching of the first half is on greatness in the kingdom, the second half is on forgiveness. The two are intimately connected, for the mark of real greatness is the ability to forgive. How this is seen supremely in God Himself! Therefore it must be true of all His family, for every child should bear the family likeness.

151

The Lord who makes us tremble at the thought of offending is the same God who calls us to show His compassion to those who do offend and to seek to recover them (Matthew 18:10–14). We cannot exhaust the love of God, for there is no boundary to its outreach, no end to its patience, no limit set to the offense. His love can bear it all yet go on loving.

It is the love described in 1 Corinthians 13:4–8 (RSV): "Love is patient and kind; love is not jealous or boastful. . . . it is not irritable or resentful; it does not rejoice at wrong, but rejoices in the right. Love bears all things, believes all things, hopes all things, endures all things. Love never ends. . . ." Somehow *that* has to become the distinctive mark of all God's children.

As we consider the lessons in the remainder of Matthew 18, look first at the instructions given in verses 15–20. This ultimately provokes the question from Peter (verses 21, 22) and leads to the parable in the final verses.

Peter's question was, "Lord how oft shall my brother sin against me, and I forgive him? . . ." The words "against me" do not appear in some manuscripts. Our responsibility to our brother is not created because he has hurt *us*, but because he has hurt *himself*. When speaking to another about his fault, it is very important that our motives be right and based upon what the Scriptures say about checking our friend concerning his error. Is it because my pride is injured, or is it because he has hurt himself and my love for him is prompting me? Think hard upon the answer to this question before acting as judge or corrector.

In any event, your concern is to gain your brother (Matthew 18:15), that is, to return him to the right path in order that he may continue to be used by the Lord. This recovery starts when you show him his fault—alone. This is not advice or permission, but an instruction from the Lord Jesus Himself. It is not easy to follow, because our human instinct, alas, is to go first to another person and discuss this friend's faults. It is only weakness or false piety that prevents us going directly to a brother (or sister) in order to point out his fault and seek to restore him.

Our business is to show him his fault, and if he acknowledges it from the depths of his soul, then the purpose of our ministry has been fulfilled. Out of that confession comes repentance, and out of repentance new fellowship with the Lord and one another.

Suppose he will not listen, what then? The responsibility is still ours, and we are to take along with us one or two others to bring him back to fellowship. But suppose he continues to be rebellious? Then we are to tell the church, for in so doing, either he will be restored, or he will be treated as a "tax collector" and put out of fellowship.

Notice clearly the responsibility that Christ places on His Church and the authority He gives it:

> Verily I say unto you, Whatsoever ye shall bind on earth shall be bound in heaven: and whatsoever ye shall loose on earth shall be loosed in heaven. Again I say unto you, that if two of you shall agree on earth as touching any thing that they shall ask, it shall be done for them of my Father which is in heaven. For where two or three are gathered together in my name, there am I in the midst of them.
>
> Matthew 18:18–20

No doubt you have often found comfort in the last two verses, but have you ever stopped to study them in their real setting? Of course, they tell us plainly that where even two or three meet in His Name, He is there; that is the Church—anywhere. They also tell us that if even two agree on some matter, it will be done by His Father, and that is the authority of the prayer meeting. Note in this context, however, there must be absolute oneness and openness between those who pray together, otherwise it is a farce, and no answer can be expected from heaven.

These verses also tell us that what the Church looses on earth is loosed in heaven. In other words, the church that agrees, pleads, and recognizes the authority of Christ in its midst has power to bind and to set free. These terse words expose the shallowness of much of our praying. How seldom we dare to besiege heaven with our requests, and therefore how little we really know about the glory of having prayer abundantly answered.

Let us look again at this section: Here is an offending brother. A friend goes to him personally, but he will not listen. So two other friends are taken along to speak to him, but he still will not hear. Finally the man is taken before the church, and the whole body takes the matter to the court of heaven, where the final authority is given either to bind or to set free. If the man listens, then the church is to receive him as the father received the prodigal son. If, however, the offender refuses to listen, then the purity of the church is most important and the unrepentant soul cannot be sheltered, but must be put outside the fellowship.

Is that the end? No! The moment he is outside, he becomes the man for whom Christ died, whom He came to seek and to save, because such a man is lost. He is denied fellowship in order that he may think things out and consent to the righteous sentence given against him, for the purity of the family of God must come first. This will make him conscious of his need and of the abundant grace of God.

These are Christ's instructions. In such circumstances, have we heeded and obeyed them?

Peter went on to say, "Lord, how often shall I forgive my brother who sins against me? As many as seven times?"

Then Jesus said to him, "I say not unto thee, Until seven times: but, Until seventy times seven" (Matthew 18:21, 22). Here we see Peter's mistake—and often it is ours as well. I am sure he thought he was being very gracious when he suggested that he might forgive seven times! In contrast with the teaching of the scribes, Peter was certainly going the extra mile.

How smug we can be with our pettiness and hurt pride, thinking we are so generous when we grudgingly say to someone, "Of course, I forgive you," when probably we would think many times before even forgiving a second time! In contrast to some of us, Peter was indeed magnanimous.

Yet what did the Lord say? "Seven times? Peter, I never said that, but I suggest you try seventy times seven—490 times!"

In other words, in Christ's kingdom, among His family, there should be no limit at all in the forgiveness of others. The man who offends is to be firmly handled, but there is to be no limit beyond which he is regarded as unrecoverable and unforgivable.

That is the principle upon which every one of us met the Lord Jesus at Calvary and were received into the Lord's church. It is the principle of all His dealings with us, and therefore it must be the principle of all our dealings with others. The Lord had already spoken about forgiveness in the Sermon on the Mount: "For if ye forgive men their trespasses, your heavenly Father will also forgive you: But if ye forgive not men their trespasses, neither will your Father forgive your trespasses" (Matthew 6:14, 15). An unforgiving spirit betrays a person who has never himself known forgiveness.

Have you suffered unjustly at the hands of someone you thought was a friend—and maybe more than once? What has been your reaction? Either you have refused to forgive, saying, "I cannot take it again!" Or you have realized that there were no limits to the insults, pain, misunderstanding, and all the rest that Jesus endured for your salvation, and therefore you dare set no limits to your forgiveness. Remember, too, that difficult people, those who make it so hard to show a forgiving spirit, are the very means the Lord is using to drive you to Calvary.

A dear friend of mine, who was for years a missionary in Colombia, South America, until he had to return home because of acute eye problems, recently sent me these verses written from his own learning experience with the Lord. He entitled it "Stumbling Blocks to Stepping-stones."

> The Christian life is like a walk
>> with Christ, our precious Lord.
> We seek to know and do His will,
>> obedient to His word.
>
> I was surprised, then, when I found
>> strewn all along the way,
> Stumbling blocks, both wide and high,
>> placed so I'd fall or stray.
>
> I asked God why, and He replied
>> in answer to my call:
> "The devil throws those stumbling blocks;
>> he wants to make you fall!
>
> "My purposes are quite distinct:
>> to change, by My great might
> Your stumbling blocks to stepping-stones,
>> and lift you from your plight!"
>
> And, thus, each stumbling block may be
>> a stepping-stone we tread,
> For God can change those stones to stairs,
>> to lift us up, instead.

> When all is grim, we know that He
>   will change, before He's done,
> Our tragedies to triumphs bright,
>   and make us like His Son!
>
> CHARLES WILLOUGHBY

The example given by the Master in the final paragraph of Matthew 18 is both simple and challenging. Notice how much the servant owed the king—ten thousand talents, which was more than fifteen years' wages of a laborer! It was an amount impossible for him to pay, but the king was moved with compassion, and in answer to the man's pleading, forgave him the debt.

That is exactly how the Lord has dealt with us. Our sins were innumerable and our debt immeasurable. No amount of "good living" on our part can ever pay the debt. Nothing we could do in the future could cover the past or atone for sin, so it is futile for us to think of squaring ourself with God for the enormity of our sin. There is only one hope:

> Not the labour of my hands
>   Can fulfil Thy law's demands;
> Could my zeal no respite know,
>   Could my tears forever flow,
> All for sin could not atone;
>   Thou must save, and Thou alone.
>
> AUGUSTUS M. TOPLADY

The debt was too big, the load too heavy, but Jesus paid it all, praise His Name! And when, utterly helpless, I came to Him, He forgave me freely on the basis of having paid the price in His own precious blood.

To return to the parable, no sooner was the servant forgiven than he found an underservant who owed him about the amount of a day's wage, and he put him in prison for it. Before you blame the man, think how Christ forgave you a debt that was enormous, yet so often you and I refuse to forgive a brother or sister some petty injury. Oh, yes, it may have hurt or harmed you, or caused you agony of mind. But in the light of Calvary, it is as a few cents against millions of dollars.

When the king heard about this, what did he do? He rescinded the pardon, put his servant in prison, and forced him to face his own tremendous debt—in fact, he was tormented ". . . till he should pay all his debt. So also my heavenly Father will do to every one of you, if you do not forgive your brother from your heart" (Matthew 18:34, 35 RSV). The last three words, "from your heart," form the keystone to the passage, for they explain again why we should never count the number of times we forgive. Because the man in the parable refused to forgive his brother, he thereby revealed that he never grasped the greatness of the king's forgiveness.

Notice again the two basic characteristics of all God's people: First, we must not dally with sin in our own lives that might cause a brother to sin also, because the punishment for that is dire (Matthew 18:5–9). Second, we must show unceasing concern toward a brother who is a sinner, in our efforts to restore him. To fail there causes us to be dealt with in awesome severity by God Himself. The one thing He will not overlook is an unforgiving spirit. For a Christian to be merciless is one of the worst of all sins, yet we see it all the time in our fellowships. We have a gospel of forgiveness for the sinner, but none for our brother or sister who stumbles.

The only evidence before heaven and earth that we truly have received mercy at God's hand is that we extend it without limit to others. If our hearts are rejoicing in His mercy to us, we will be merciful to others. A speaker at the English Keswick Convention once said, "We do not receive God's forgiveness in a cup, but in a pipe-line." Think of that! Our ability to forgive comes not from our own meager supply, but from Calvary itself.

This has been a difficult message, but if we are to climb on track with the Lord Jesus, it is a lesson that must be learned, put into daily practice, and obeyed continually. Prove your own forgiveness by the way you treat your brothers and sisters in Christ. As Paul said, "Be ye kind one to another, tenderhearted, forgiving one another, even as God for Christ's sake hath forgiven you" (Ephesians 4:32).

Impossible? Yes, in our own, natural strength, but it is wonderfully possible for the Holy Spirit who indwells us, because the fruit of the Spirit is *love.*

20

The Terms of Discipleship

Discipline is the quality that makes or breaks a prospective mountain climber. Those who aim to tackle what few others dare to do must be special people who understand the meaning of self-discipline and have the capacity to be disciplined by others. "Can two walk together, except they be agreed?" (Amos 3:3) is a rhetorical question that applies to every relationship in life, whether it be membership in an expedition, the lifelong relationship of marriage, or devotion to the Lord Jesus Christ.

I make no apology for using such words as *discipleship, discipline,* and *obedience* over and over, because that is what Christian living is all about. The terms of discipleship were laid down by Christ Himself in Luke 14:25–33. We will study them in reverse order to the way the Lord spoke them.

The Lord gave two illustrations of what we often call "counting the cost" in verses 28–32. First, there was a builder who had to reckon carefully the material required in building a tower, as a quantity surveyor does. How humiliating to get near the top and find insufficient bricks! Then there was a king going out to battle, who assessed his forces in relation to those coming against him, for defeat must not be in his reckoning.

What does Jesus say about these situations? That the builder should order more bricks or that the king should train more soldiers? Not exactly. "Count the cost" means that we must give up all that we have in order to fulfill what the Lord demands: "So likewise, whosoever he be of you that forsaketh not all that he hath, he cannot be my disciple" (Luke 14:33).

There is no thought here of mere cost accounting to see if the material is adequate or that the armed forces are sufficient. We do not yield to the Lord Jesus just enough of our lives to accomplish what has to be done. He demands that we completely renounce all that we consider our own, in order that He might give us the resources we need. His own resources are always adequate for every demand made upon us—nothing less than the life and power of the indwelling Holy Spirit.

We may look at our bank account and think we can give a certain amount to Christian work. Is this counting the cost? Indeed, it is not! If we are lucky enough to possess a bank account, every cent in it belongs to the Lord Jesus, and we are His stewards to use it at His direction. We renounce our claim to it, just as we do to our lives. All that we have, we hold for Him. Then, because He has first claim, far from being bereft of anything, we experience the lavishness of His supply.

I do not mean this in financial terms necessarily, for there is nothing in Scripture to encourage us to believe that obedience to the Lord makes us materially rich. But if we give Him our all—our selves, our resources, our families and homes—then He has promised we ". . . shall receive a hundredfold. . ." (Mark 10:30). The supreme glory of this exchange is that we experience in a new way the joy of His smile and the blessing of His ungrieved presence.

In 1 Chronicles 4:23 (RSV) a group of people are mentioned who were potters and ". . . dwelt there with the king for his work." It is possible for God's people either to live with their work for the King, or to live with the King for His work. To adopt the former attitude is to live with all of our own inadequacies; to live with the King for His work is to have all the resources which are at His command.

"Whosoever doth not bear his cross, and come after me, cannot be my disciple," Jesus said in Luke 14:27. What does it mean to bear your own cross? There are many queer ideas about cross bearing. I recall a man once saying to me, "I have a fierce temper, but I suppose that is my cross!"

"My friend," I said to him (lovingly, I hope!). "That is not your cross. It is your wife's cross, but it is your sin!"

What was the cross in the life of Jesus? He came down to Earth in human form to live a blameless life, to "do good," and by signs and wonders reveal to those who had eyes to see that He was indeed the Anointed One of God. But there was still something more He had to do, and that was yield His body. This He did on the cross at Calvary. For it was in His body that He bore our sin (*see* 1 Peter 2:24), and in that same body He was raised from the grave and ascended into heaven.

So now, said Paul in Romans 6:13, ". . . yield yourselves unto God, as those that are alive from the dead, and your members [body] as instruments of righteousness unto God." This, however, is not a once-for-all act (although when we realize that is what is expected of us, it is a crisis), but it is followed by a daily commitment, for Paul writes again, ". . . present your bodies a living sacrifice, holy, acceptable unto God . . ." (Romans 12:1).

Bishop Taylor-Smith was chaplain in chief of the British armed forces during World War I and later a missionary in West Africa. It is said of him that every morning when he awakened, he would stretch himself on his bed (and he was a very large man!) and say, "Lord, for today, this bed is my altar, my body the sacrifice; Your orders, please!" What a way to start the day! May we all find this the pattern for our commitment. Not only our resources, but our *bodies* at the Lord's disposal.

Paul was not giving advice that he himself was unwilling to take. In 1 Corinthians 9:27 he wrote, "I keep under my body, and bring it into subjection: lest that by any means, when I have preached to others, I myself should be a castaway." Do you and I know anything at all about discipline like that? It is in the same stream of self-denial in which the Lord Jesus endured the cross because of the joy that He knew awaited Him (*see* Hebrews 12:2). He gave Himself, His body, His all to accomplish our salvation. How far has our individual response to Him led us?

Let us turn back to the opening words that the Lord spoke in Luke 14:26, "If any man come to me, and hate not his father, and mother, and wife, and children, and brethren, and sisters, yea, and his own life also, he cannot be my disciple."

This is one of Jesus' most difficult sayings, because it seems to go against so many other things He taught. Some commentators try to explain that when the Lord said *hate*, He did not mean it in the way we use the word, but rather that in comparison with our love for Him, our feelings for those closest to us should be as hate. This so-called explanation seems to me even harder to understand. No, for He had told us to love our neighbors as ourselves, and Paul wrote, "Husbands, love your wives, even as Christ also loved the church . . ." (Ephesians 5:25).

To understand this passage it is necessary to be clear about the meaning of the word *hate,* which is used also in Romans 9:13 and is a quote from Malachi 1:2, 3, "Jacob have I loved, but Esau have I hated." The emphasis of the word is not hatred, but rejection: "Jacob I loved, but Esau I rejected."

Imagine the director of a business who, during his working hours, controls the affairs of his firm. When he comes home, does he start issuing orders to his wife and family? He had better not! At that point he "rejects" his role of business executive and becomes a loving husband and father in the family.

Does this throw light upon the words of the Lord Jesus? Reject your family ties and even your own life in order to put Him first; that is what He has been saying all along! Now He uses even stronger words to emphasize the fact that for His people to be utterly fulfilled and satisfied, He *must* have first place in their affections, their thoughts, their daily living. Such people, and those alone, may call themselves His disciples.

A *disciple* is the word used for any person who follows closely a teacher. When a person is born again of the Spirit of God, he is just a spiritual baby, yet a disciple. His growth occurs as he recognizes the Lordship of Christ and puts Him first in every area of life.

Unless that is so, the Lord said, a person is not, and cannot be, one of His disciples. Strong words, but the Lord cannot have half-hearted followers, who are unreliable, likely at any moment to backslide, and whose lives never reveal the fruit of the Spirit. No wonder the world looks upon such people askance and says "If *that* is a Christian, I do not want to be one!" What a bitter indictment upon unholy living, because shame, dishonor and ridicule are brought upon the name of Christ!

To see clearly what sort of person the Lord wants at His side, how He expects him to live, and the reason why He has such a high standard, we read in John 20:21, ". . . As my Father hath sent me, even so send I you."

Here is something much more than merely a comparison of purpose. There is also similarity in the *way* in which the Father sent the Son and the way in which the Son sends His disciples. The whole desire of God is that we might enter into the same *way* of being sent that we see in the Lord Jesus. The comparison is fourfold and must be studied carefully as we consider the nature of discipleship.

First, therefore, notice that our Lord was not sent into the world alone. In John 14:10, 11 He said, "Believest thou not that I am in the Father, and the Father in me?" The Father sent Him into the world identified with Himself, and we see the effect of that relationship in the remainder of the verse: "The words that I speak unto you, I speak not of myself: but the Father that dwelleth in me, he doeth the works."

In the allegory of the vine in John 15, because the branch is in the vine, the life of the vine is in the branch. In that way the Father and Son were united and so is the Lord and His disciple. A. J. Gordon wrote, "We do not stand in the world bearing witness to Christ; but we stand in Christ, bearing witness to the world." That is the secret of power.

Second, when the Father sent the Son into the world, the Son was helpless in Himself, for He said, ". . . The Son can do nothing of his own accord, but only what he sees the Father doing; for whatever he does, that the Son does likewise. . . . I can do nothing on my own authority . . ." (John 5:19, 30 RSV). Even the sinless humanity of our blessed Lord profited nothing.

When the Lord came into this world, utterly helpless in His humanity, He was none the less God than He was before. The One who had been God from all eternity voluntarily laid aside the use of every attribute of deity and assumed a complete human nature without sin.

When we turn to ourselves, the parallel is obvious. We have to assent to the Lord's verdict upon us: "Without *me* ye can do nothing" (John 15:5, *italics mine*). As the Father sent Him, so He has sent us, completely helpless in ourselves. Any work we do except in the energy of the Holy Spirit is the fruit of our own sinfulness. The essence of sin is independence, whereas the genius of Christian experience is dependence. "I can do all things," Paul said, *"through Christ* who strengthens me."

Every work of my hands that is not under the control of God's Holy Spirit is simply breeding more sin. How can God, whose eyes can look upon nothing that is impure, look upon the work of His servants, if the work is done in self-effort, no matter how good the motives?

Our activity shows we are made in the image of the first man, who was of the earth. But there is a second Man, the Lord from heaven, who longs to move in and replace us with Himself, so that we may dare to say, "The words that I speak and the things that I do come no longer from myself. The Christ who indwells me, He does the works." That is God's plan.

Evangelism that does not flow from this principle simply spreads carnality. A fellowship of believers who are not living in revival must first get right with God and then, in His strength, seek to lead others to Him and help them grow in faith and spiritual knowledge.

Third, the redemptive purpose of God was accomplished by the Father living in the Son by the agency of the Holy Spirit. The power of the indwelling Father and Spirit was given without measure to the Son. "*So* send I you," the Lord Jesus said. And He gives Himself without measure to us, "For he whom God has sent utters the words of God, for it is not by measure that he gives the Spirit" (John 3:34 RSV).

The Lord requires only one thing from you and me, and that is what He Himself gave to His Father: complete, full consent. The moment I give my commitment, I begin to experience the amazing wonder that I am sent with the complete sufficiency of the indwelling, glorified Christ, who is in control, shedding abroad His Holy Spirit, giving Himself without measure to my yielded heart. This is how the Lord Jesus lived here on Earth, as the Father gave Himself without measure to His yielded, obedient Son. Let us all get this very clearly in our minds and hearts, for if we do not experience this infilling, then we merely serve the Lord within the limitations of our own insufficiency and collapse under the strain.

Finally, when the Father sent His Son into the world, it was necessary for the Son to be crucified before He could complete the mission for which He had been sent. "Truly, truly I say to you, unless a grain of wheat falls into the earth and dies, it remains alone; but if it dies, it bears much fruit" (John 12:24 RSV). These tremendous words have affected the lives of all mankind ever since they were spoken. If the Son had not been crucified, He would have remained alone, and you and I would be lost. The Father sent the Son by the way of the cross. So if I am to accomplish the mission upon which the Lord sends me, I, too, must know the meaning of crucifixion. There is no detour, no way to argue or debate it. No one denies that the Son had to die, therefore we cannot deny that we also must die.

When the resurrected Lord showed His astonished disciples His wounds (John 20:20), they knew that their future path was to be the way of self-crucifixion. The only thing that could have hindered God's purpose of redemption from being accomplished would have been the refusal of His Son to die on the cross. The one thing that can prevent God's purpose in my life and your life is our refusal to die on that cross. If I die, all is victory; if I live, there is nothing but loss. Jesus said, "He that loveth his life shall lose it; and he that hateth his life in this world shall keep it unto life eternal" (John 12:25).

What was the destination of Jesus when He left heaven? It was certainly not Bethlehem. Had He reached His destination when He came to Calvary? No, that was but another stop on the journey— the most important one, because without it nothing else could have been accomplished. After the cross came a tomb, but that was not His destination, because He arose triumphant and returned to heaven in His physical body. Was that His destination? Not entirely, because He said, "... It is expedient for you that I go away: for if I go not away, the Comforter will not come unto you ..." (John 16:7). This was His destination—that He might come to indwell you and me and all those who call upon Him in repentance and faith.

The purpose of redemption is fulfilled in the heart of God only when He is in control of men and women by the power of the Holy Spirit. Such people can be trusted anywhere. Their lives no longer belong to them, for they have gladly been yielded to Him who fills them with all the fullness of the Godhead bodily. These are true disciples, the sheep who closely follow the Shepherd, who hear His voice and obey.

A crucified Lord seeks crucified people, for it is only such people who can share His burden for a lost world. Are you one whom He can trust and use?

21

The Victory of Love

Less than an hour's drive from my home is one of the most beautiful parts of Britain, the Lake District. That is where the English Keswick Convention began over one hundred years ago, in the little market town of Keswick. Craggy hills and mountains, often rising sheer from the lakes, offer walking and climbing delights for many people. In some rugged areas, the world's best-known climbers practice various aspects of the sport.

The mountains also furnish a pleasure ground for ramblers and scramblers. These latter can be a menace. Often people take to the hills with inadequate clothing; some wear tennis shoes or sneakers, and women even go up the rugged paths in high-heeled shoes. They never inquire about the weather, which they should, because at times, without warning, a mist can sweep in off the Irish Sea and envelop the area in dense, wet fog, in which the inexperienced lose their sense of direction completely.

Because many hikers never tell anyone where they plan to go, only when they fail to return to their friends or to the hostel where they were staying is the alert sounded. Then the Mountain Rescue Team must spend many hours—and perhaps much money—in rescuing the lost party. Everywhere there are warnings about careless mountain walking and the dangers involved, but these warnings are too often ignored. The safety factor is not considered by the careless, yet a few words with those who are experienced and wise could save them much trouble and danger.

In Acts 2 we need to take notice of the missing factor in much of modern church life. The wisdom of those who follow the ways of the Lord contrasts sharply with those who try to be clever and trendy, yet fail to reach the summit with God.

The closing verse of Acts 2 says, ". . . And the Lord added to the church daily such as should be saved" (verse 47). The New English Bible puts it this way, "Day by day the Lord added to their number those whom he was saving." Saving is something that the Lord Himself does; in the exercise of His sovereign will, He Himself brings it to pass.

Jesus did the adding, because conditions within the infant church were God honoring and called forth a demonstration of His power in fulfillment of John 14:12, where He said, "Verily, verily, I say unto you, He that believeth on me, the works that I do shall he do also; and greater works than these shall he do; because I go unto my Father." What a victory!

Greater works? What are these? Does that mean a few more raised from the dead like Lazarus (only to die again)? No, surely the greater works are accomplished through ordinary men and women living in touch with God by the power of the indwelling Spirit and being used to transform other lives into the likeness of Christ. There can be no greater work on earth than that!

Eagerly, almost wistfully, we bend our will and open our heart to the ministry of the Holy Spirit and cry, "O God, do it again today! Show us why revival has not happened in our time, and then give us grace to remedy the wrong!"

The second chapter of Acts describes the birth of the most amazing society the world has ever known. It had none of the trappings we consider essential—no committees, no talented leadership (because in the main they were "uneducated, common men," according to Acts 4:13 [RSV]), without financial resources. The church was born amidst hostile people who could command vast material power, sufficient to crush the whole venture before its impact could be felt.

These early believers had little doctrine; it followed later to explain their experience, whereas today we have much doctrine with little experience to be explained. Yet in that young church were centered all the hopes of God—the Father, the Son, and the Holy Spirit—and through it His purposes for the world were to be fulfilled. For the formation of this society, Jesus had given Himself on the cross. Now the Holy Spirit had come to live in the heart of every member of Christ's Body, that He might direct, control, and guide.

If Jesus Christ's hopes were not to be disappointed, God's purposes not to be frustrated, what do you consider must be the one quality His people must possess? If the Church is really to be a power in the world, to influence and even shape the future course of history, what must it have above everything else?

To answer that question, let me ask another: What quality was lacking in the lives of those through whom God was seeking to fulfill His purpose in Old Testament days? Where had men failed? Listen to the analysis of the Lord Jesus, in answer to a question put to Him: "Thou shalt love the Lord thy God with all thy heart, and with all thy soul, and with all thy mind. This is the first and great commandment. And the second is like unto it, Thou shalt love thy neighbour as thyself. On these two commandments hang all the law and the prophets" (Matthew 22:37–40).

Where was the point of breakdown? *Love!* God had commanded it right from His early dealings with men, for Jesus was quoting from the Law given in Leviticus and Deuteronomy. Jesus emphasized it again and again to His disciples, "A new commandment I give unto you, That ye love one another; as I have loved you, that ye also love one another. By this shall all men know that ye are my disciples, if ye have love one to another" (John 13:34, 35).

The all-important question Jesus asked Peter when he was discouraged over his failure was, ". . . Do you love *me. . . ?*" John 21:15–17 RSV, *italics mine*). Years later, Peter wrote for us to read, ". . . Add to your faith . . . *love*" (*see* 2 Peter 1:5, 7), and Paul, under the control of the Holy Spirit, penned 1 Corinthians 13, which culminates in the thought that the greatest of all the virtues is *love.*

Pentecost marked the entrance into the world of something never known before. Now, as generation upon generation of believers come and go, each one needs to confront the world with God's love which ". . . is shed abroad in our hearts by the Holy Ghost which is given unto us" (Romans 5:5). It is the one quality that is essential in the life of every individual Christian, but which, alas, is so often lacking.

The truly influential church is the church governed, not only by intellectual ability, but by Holy Spirit love in the heart of each member. Gifts certainly have their place, but love is God's eternal dynamic, which the world needs so desperately to feel. Such love is not patronizing affection or mere courtesy or affability, but a concern that is deep and significant. It is the word used in John 3:16 (*italics mine*), "God *so* loved. . . ." It is the love of God Himself, a love that hurts and costs and gives its all. If you want to see it in all its power, look at the cross.

This love of God was liberated at Pentecost to be the greatest factor in evangelism throughout church history, because love's action at Calvary led to the coming of the Holy Spirit. If you read the whole of Acts 2, you see it in operation in the church and its effect upon the world.

Notice first the characteristics of a love-filled church: "And they continued stedfastly in the apostles' doctrine and fellowship, and in breaking of bread, and in prayers" (Acts 2:42). Here was love for the Word of God, which caused His people to return to it again and again. A love for one another is seen in utter selflessness, and a love for the Lord in the breaking of bread from house to house, combined with a love for prayer. They were really "together" (*see* verses 44–46). Togetherness starts in being at one around the Throne of God. It never grows in a self-centered group, but only when each Christian has a desire to share his faith and mutual concern with others.

Here was the victory of love in the church, the *koinonia,* the love that lies at the heart of the Christian message. A fellowship of believers does not demand sentiment, but first devotion and then discipline. Yes, we are back to that word again! But if we are to be climbers and not scramblers, then we must abide by the rules. As soldiers in the Lord's army, His people have to learn to "keep rank," because in the constant battle with evil, we need to be always on the alert. No one can do just what he likes all of the time or what he would do if he were on his own. It means our own opinions, views, and preferences have to be given up occasionally.

Some Christians never realize that cooperation is necessary, and they want to be individualists all the time, so that if their views are not accepted, they step out of rank. We are not asked to agree with everyone all the time, but as followers of the Lord Jesus, we should find it possible to disagree and to do it agreeably. Dr. Vance Havner once said, "When the tide is out, every little shrimp has its own puddle. But when the tide comes in—!" That is the answer, the tide of Holy Spirit love.

Fellowship in the church corrects any exaggerated ideas we may have of our own importance. Opinions and preferences, often due to prejudice, are removed as they are submitted to the disciplines of fellowship. You may not agree with every action your church decides to take. The whole church *could* be wrong and you right, but it shows a marked lack of humility to assume that without very prayerful thought. It is more likely to be God's way of showing you that your view is not so important after all, and He calls on you to glorify Him by submitting to the discipline of fellowship and letting love conquer by keeping rank.

The Christian who exerts the most influence in the church is the one who knows the difference between vital truth and personal opinion. As a result, he gives in quietly on matters of opinion in order to keep rank with the rest. Then, when some matter of vital truth is concerned, he is heard with respect, for he is known as one whose first concern is the glory of God.

That is the victory of love revealed in Acts 2:42, 45, 46: love for God's Word, love for each other, love for the Lord. The *koinonia* the Lord gave His people started here, in a love-filled fellowship. Because of this, there was a twofold consequence upon those outside the fellowship, those in the world. Something happened on earth, and something happened in heaven (verse 43): "And fear came upon every soul: and many wonders and signs were done by the apostles."

Here was a church to be feared! That sense of awe and conviction that grips the heart of an unbeliever in the presence of a community filled with the power of the Holy Spirit was an immediate evidence of God's presence. Does such a sense of awe confront strangers who come into your church? Such an experience of the Spirit's power would assure reality in our worship and make people almost afraid to come inside, lest they be converted.

> And great fear came upon all the church, and upon as many as heard these things. And by the hands of the apostles were many signs and wonders wrought among the people. . . . And of the rest durst no man join himself to them; but the people magnified them. And believers were the more added to the Lord. . . .
>
> Acts 5:11–14

The signs and wonders were the evidence of the supernatural working of God's Spirit, the consequence of heaven's favor upon a fellowship filled with His love.

Then we read of those early believers "praising God, and having favour with all the people . . ." (Acts 2:47). Fear . . . favor! A strange combination, but how wonderful! The persecution of the church did not come from the ordinary people, but from religious leaders—and that is always true. Counterfeit religion is always the greatest enemy of the truth. The early church, filled with Holy Spirit love which flowed through to the world, found favor with the people.

Such a church does not have to seek the world's patronage, nor create slick programs to entice the unwilling through the church doors. Once you lose love—the love of God, love for God, love for others—then you lose the people, for you have lost the magnetism of Calvary. To descend to other levels in a frantic attempt to keep up the statistics is a confession that the power of love is missing, because there is no substitute for Holy Spirit love.

Conversely, when love shines through, wrongs are righted, the strong are strengthened, the lonely find fellowship, the defeated find hope, and the lost find Jesus. Revival comes only to a church from which suspicion, mistrust, coldness of heart, lack of confidence, and lovelessness have departed.

Then, and only then, something happened in heaven: The Lord added to the church daily those who were being saved (*see* Acts 2:47). This started in verse 41: ". . . The same day there were added unto them about three thousand souls." It happened again in Acts 5:14, "Believers were the more added to the Lord. . . ," and in Acts 6:7, ". . . The number of the disciples multiplied in Jerusalem greatly. . . ."

They were added to the church, but primarily added to the Lord Himself. The *Lord* did it—not their eloquence or efficiency. He added day by day to His own Body. Wherever He can find a love-filled fellowship, He will do it again today. The attitude of those outside Christ is negative because of our lack of love. They are scrambling, when they could be climbing! They have no clothing or equipment adequate for the demands of life, though it is all available for them in Jesus Christ.

Christians have lost favor with the people because they have lost their quality of love, and they have lost that because they have forgotten the meaning of true fellowship. People say the church has lost touch with the world, but that is not so. The tragedy is that the church has lost touch with God and therefore has lost her drawing power.

This can be restored only by taking positive action to restore fellowship when and where it has been broken, to keep in rank with others, to sink personal preferences, to put right whatever each individual knows is wrong in his or her own life. All of this is possible only as we get alone with God and ask Him to shed abroad His love in our hearts.

Our sick society could be transformed to a heaven on earth very quickly if *love* got through. This is God's will for His children, and He has made it possible through the Holy Spirit for us to love as He loved.

22

The Light of His Return

A major mountaineering event occurred in 1953. The first two men finally reached the summit of Mount Everest. Sir Edmund Hillary and Tenzing Norkay posed to take their own pictures up there on the snow under brilliant blue skies, standing where no man had ever stood before. They had conquered the world's highest peak and, because they had arrived at the summit and survived, the world rejoiced. How jubilant were all the members of their expedition! Two made the final assault, but all their companions rejoiced.

Jesus Christ is the only Man who achieved the spiritual summit, heaven. He was the first of a new generation, and those who know and love Him are being formed into His likeness, one day to share His triumph. We will meet Him; we will be with Him; we shall see His face! What joy, what rejoicing, what triumph! May the very thought of it keep us on track, heading also for that summit of final union with Him.

Some of us may not have to go through the valley of the shadow of death to see our Savior. The most tremendous event yet to come upon this earth might take place during our lifetime—the coming again in power and glory of the Lord Jesus.

Lest some might think this is just a "pie in the sky" philosophy, let me remind you that the "blessed hope" of the Lord's personal and bodily return is one of the major emphases in the New Testament. Out of the twenty-seven books, there is specific reference to it in twenty-three, and of the other four, Galatians is the longest, while the others are Philemon, 2 and 3 John—each containing only one chapter. This *hope* was the inspiration of the ministry of the early believers, the flaming passion of their evangelism, the burning motive for a holy life.

The words of the Lord Jesus continued to ring in the ears of His disciples, ". . . I will come again . . ." (John 14:3). Many of His parables also pictured this great event. Because they lived looking for His return, the early Christians experienced a sense of urgency to accomplish the job of world evangelism, so that it was said by their enemies, ". . . These that have turned the world upside down are come hither also" (Acts 17:6).

Could that be said of twentieth-century Christians of your church fellowship, of your own life? Or have the centuries since our Lord ascension dulled our anticipation of His promised return? If so, we urgently need to reconsider living in the light of His return as we head for the summit of union with Him. "Our commonwealth is in heaven, and from it we await a Savior, the Lord Jesus Christ, who will change our lowly body to be like his glorious body, by the power which enables him even to subject all things to himself" (Philippians 3:20, 21 RSV).

If ever we needed a revival of this hope in our hearts, with all its implications for our service and sanctification, it is today. Because to God a thousand years are as a day, the promise of His return was given but yesterday in His calendar! Peter said that God ". . . is not slack concerning his promise, . . . but is longsuffering to us-ward, not willing that any should perish, but that all should come to repentance" (2 Peter 3:9).

World conditions today are absolutely terrifying. A decade ago the word on everyone's lips was *enlightenment;* now it is *survival.* There is the threat of nuclear war, and nothing seems able to prevent it. The world's hope a few years ago centered in the United Nations, but its efforts at world peace have become a mockery in Israel, Southeast Asia, Afghanistan, and every country where it has attempted to avoid war.

Political thought moves rapidly toward a world with one man in control. Of course, this is not new, because Alexander the Great, Napoleon, and Adolf Hitler all had the same idea. They foresaw world power headed by one man, but each sought to be that man. Communism aims at that today and holds a third of the world in its grasp. But where is the man? Everybody waits!

The Christian, however, has the answer: the Man at God's right hand. In spite of the rage of the heathen and people who imagine vain things, the Lord says, "Yet have I set my king upon my holy hill of Zion" (*see* Psalms 2:1–6). One of the closing announcements in the Bible is that when an angel sounded his trumpet, loud voices in heaven declared, ". . . The kingdoms of this world are become the kingdoms of our Lord, and of his Christ; and he shall reign for ever and ever" (Revelation 11:15).

He is the only one who can rule in righteousness, and the present situation cries out for it. The Bible speaks of the certainty of Christ's coming, and the whole emphasis of the New Testament is on that tremendous hope.

Furthermore, the New Testament indicates certain conditions that will be prevailing when Jesus comes. No one knows the hour, so be careful of calendars and timetables: "Watch therefore: for ye know not what hour your Lord doth come" (Matthew 24:42). However, there are indications of a world at war (*see* Matthew 24:7). There is no hint of a gradual betterment until world civilization emerges into a Utopia, but rather a steady decline. Christians will be hated, we are told: "Then shall they deliver you up to be afflicted, and shall kill you: and ye shall be hated of all nations for my name's sake" (Matthew 24:9). Also, the church will be corrupted with much false teaching, "And because iniquity shall abound, the love of many shall wax cold" (Matthew 24:12).

How true all this is today! I am told on good authority that in the average evangelical church in Western society, of the total membership roll, 5 percent do not exist, 10 percent cannot be found, 25 percent never attend church, 50 percent have no missionary interest, 75 percent have never attended midweek service and prayer meeting, 90 percent have no family worship at home, and 95 percent never win anyone to Christ. If these figures are in any way true, how can we ever evangelize society with a church so indifferent and often so fragmented?

On the other hand, as Matthew 24:14 says, there will be a revival of missionary interest before the Lord's coming, but at the same time there will be a whole multitude of people who are indifferent (Matthew 24:38, 39). All these circumstances exist today.

"But," you may ask, *"how* will Jesus come?"

The Scriptures leave us in no doubt. "This same Jesus . . . shall so come in like manner as ye have seen him go into heaven" (Acts 1:11). "For the Lord himself shall descend from heaven with a shout, with the voice of the archangel, and with the trump of God . . ." (1 Thessalonians 4:16).

One thing is very obvious—His coming will be dramatic and unexpected, like a thief in the night. It will be universal and powerful: "Then shall two be in the field. . . . Two women shall be grinding at the mill; the one shall be taken, and the other left" (Matthew 24:40, 41). And Luke adds that two will be in a bed, one taken and the other left (*see* Luke 17:34, 35). In other words, Christ's coming will be at midnight somewhere, early morning in another part of the world, and midday in yet another.

What a contrast this will be to Bethlehem! How local and how lonely His coming was then. Only a few saw the child and came to worship, and few of them understood. How few people today really know and acknowledge the One who was born at Bethlehem and understand the meaning of His coming! Surely we have a responsibility to make Him known while yet there is time.

Look further at this great subject and see what a comfort His coming is. ". . . The dead in Christ shall rise first; Then we which are alive and remain shall be caught up together with them in the clouds, to meet the Lord in the air: and so shall we ever be with the Lord. Wherefore, comfort one another with these words" (1 Thessalonians 4:16–18).

In periods of intense persecution, such as existed when Paul wrote those words, the hope of the imminent return of Christ has always been a foretaste of glory: "Looking for that blessed hope, and the glorious appearing of the great God and our Saviour Jesus Christ" (Titus 2:13).

At the time of the Lord's return, both dead and living will be united with Him. How that thought must have sustained those going through imprisonment, torture, and death for the sake of Christ! We will receive a resurrection body, and—glorious thought!—there will be no more sin or temptation. There will be no more attacks from the devil: He will be thrown into the abyss forever. There will be no more parting or sorrow or tears, and the living Lord will nourish His people from the fountain of the water of life without payment (*see* Revelation 21:3–6).

There are, however, certain consequences of His coming, and I want to point out three. First, the eternal destiny of every man and woman will be finally decided. The door that will shut some into the kingdom will shut others out (*see* Matthew 25:1–13).

Some terrifying words are found in Revelation 20:11–15, describing the judgment before the Great White Throne: "And whosoever was not found written in the book of life was cast into the lake of fire." Such teaching is regarded as medieval in these days, so there is little preaching about the reality of heaven and hell. But the Lord left us in no doubt; our prime concern must be to assure ourselves that our own names are found in His "book of life," and that we introduce others to the Savior, so that they, too, can have this certainty.

In the second place, there will be rewards for faithfulness in service: "For we must all appear before the judgment seat of Christ; that every one may receive the things done in his body, according to that he hath done, whether it be good or bad" (2 Corinthians 5:10). What we do *in our body* from day to day, our actions, and reactions, our thoughts and words, are all preparation for future service in Christ's kingdom.

That is the thrust of the parable of the talents (or pounds) in Luke 19:11–27. The Master's commendation to the faithful servant included bestowal of authority. We may not understand this now, because we are told almost nothing about life in heaven, but we know enough to realize that as God's people we cannot live uncommitted or meaningless lives.

A dear friend of mine, the man who led me to Christ, became a very high executive in business. Some years later, I met him when he was in middle life, and I had heard he was planning early retirement. When I asked, he told me that his firm had decided upon a course of action that he, as a Christian, could not condone. Therefore he had chosen to resign, because, he said, "The price in terms of eternity is too high to pay." How much do you and I understand of that principle?

My final thought on the consequences of Christ's coming is that the devil is overthrown. You can read about that great occurrence in Revelation 12:12. The whole chapter relates Satan's fierce onslaught on the Church, the "child," but in God's timetable, the devil is always too late to do the ultimate damage and destroy the Church. For the whole believing populace is caught up into heaven, and Satan is destroyed. He no longer will have power to accuse us before the Throne of God. Even now, you and I can anticipate that victory, because Satan is already a defeated foe, and he has no right to a hold on our lives. As someone has said, he may roar like a lion, but if we look closely, we can see that his teeth are drawn.

As we rejoice over the consequences of Christ's coming, we notice that there is also a continuing challenge before us. The thought that our time may be brief should cause us to concentrate on evangelism as never before. Some misguided folk, who think they have the very day of the Second Coming worked out, leave homes and work to assemble on high ground, so that they may be the first ones called into the air. The promise of His coming should not make us indolent, but spur us on to greater efforts to bring others to a saving knowledge of the Lord's grace.

Living in the light of Christ's return challenges us to the greatest task of all, as we head for the summit of seeing Jesus face to face, and that is holiness of life. If you read any passage about the Second Coming, you will see it is linked with purity of life. For example, ". . . What sort of persons ought you to be in lives of holiness and godliness, waiting for and hastening the coming of the day of God . . ." (2 Peter 3:11, 12 RSV). "Beloved, now are we the sons of God, and . . . when he shall appear, we shall be like him; for we shall see him as he is. And every man that hath this hope in him purifieth himself, even as he is pure" (1 John 3:2, 3).

Our lives should reflect the hope that we have of spending eternity in the presence of God, because that is what we are doing even here on earth. Our relationship to Him is something we should cherish and maintain in all obedience every moment of the day, so that we never bring shame on His glorious Name.

It is said that in the south of France, where many famous perfumes are made, when the workers leave the factories, the whole area is fragrant with the aroma they carry in their clothing. In the same way, the true Christian exudes the fragrance of his Lord because of his close proximity to Him.

Live daily in the light of His return! Scale the heights until you join Him on the summit, to be forever in His presence!

Epilogue

Forward and Upward

In the months and years of somewhat reduced activity and yet expanded ministry, from my meditation and observation has grown a great burden. Insofar as possible, within the limits of this book, I have sought to discharge that burden on my heart for God's people today and most of all for myself. My concluding thought is best expressed in the words of Isaiah, through whom the Lord said, "For I will pour water upon him that is thirsty, and floods upon the dry ground: I will pour my spirit upon thy seed, and my blessing upon thine offspring" (Isaiah 44:3).

One of the great perils of today is that we perceive our greatest problem to be the titanic struggle with communism (or Marxism). It is regarded as our most dangerous enemy. We equate Christianity with the free world and all that is good; all that is evil we identify as being behind the Iron Curtain. Piously we assume that God is on our side and that He is the avowed enemy of the so-called pagan nations.

However, the issue lies far deeper than that. In a word, it is the holiness of God and the sinfulness of the human heart. It is not a matter of nationalism, in which God is on our side and the devil on the other. It is rather a matter of personal repentance, for our great enemy is the evil of human character. It is not a question of outward, material foes, but rather of inward, spiritual failure. This is *the* issue with which each one of us needs to be primarily concerned today.

Some people think it inconceivable that a holy God might allow such a corrupt nation as Soviet Russia to humiliate our so-called civilized and Christianized western society. But He has done such a thing before. That was Habbakuk's problem long ago, as he saw the threat of Chaldean power confronting Israel. He did not counterattack with anti-Chaldean literature, but called Israel to repentance. The call to repentance is the vital element missing in our preaching today.

The great need of the hour is repentance toward God and forsaking of sin, individually and nationally, so that even at this desperate moment in history God may grant us mercy. Many Christians say, "The Lord is coming, and all will be well!" That is no answer. Remember how Christ said, ". . . Lift up your heads; for your redemption draweth nigh" (Luke 21:28)? He also warned us to humble ourselves, to watch and pray, and to declare war against sin in the church and out of it, that God may have mercy on us. "For," as Peter said, "the time has come for judgment to begin with the household of God . . ." (1 Peter 4:17 RSV).

Only Holy Spirit power released through a repentant people can reverse the trend of history. The great peril confronting us is not that we should be swamped by communism, but that our complacency should cut us off from the almighty power of God.

During the nine years I was pastor at Moody Memorial Church, Chicago, this burden lay heavily upon me. One of the members of the church gave me a letter that was written in D. L. Moody's own hand and was from the founder of the church to one of his elders. I have treasured it ever since, and I quote it verbatim. It was written from Baltimore and dated October 26, 1878.

My dear Brother

I have often thought of you since October 19. My heart went out to you and I have prayed often for you since that night, and my prayer is that you may be full of the Holy Spirit. Why should we not lay hold of Matthew 5:6? Surely there is a promise for us and why should we not make it real and enter into its fullness? Acts 1:8 has come to my soul over and over again and it is a mighty blessing to my soul and I trust it will be to you.

Now, do you not think it will be a good thing to get all who are hungry for the same blessing to gather once a week for prayer? I would not give it out in the meeting but get hold of them one to time [meaning "one at a time"?] and if you do not get but a few you will find it a great help to you. I hope you will not rest until you get a full blessing. God has a *mighty* blessing for you and he can use you to do a great work.

I wish you would write me often and let me know how you are getting on and tell me about the church. I do want to see that church made aglow in Chicago for good.

Remember me to all friends from your friend and brother.

D. L. Moody

Was Moody a wild Pentacostalist or extreme charismatic? Of course not! He was simply hungry for God's best. The Word of God says, "Blessed are those who hunger and thirst for righteousness, for they shall be satisfied"(Matthew 5:6 RSV).

This is also the promise of Isaiah 44:3, which prophesied that great covenant blessing of the church, the gift of the Holy Spirit. The first promise of the text, "I will pour water on the thirsty land . . . ," is explained by the second, "I will pour my Spirit upon your descendants. . . ." The Spirit is always like refreshing, life-giving water.

Now, we must realize that the Spirit has already been given, and He has never been withdrawn. He is permanently resident in the hearts of every one of God's people, yet we demonstrate little evidence of His presence. When the Spirit works, it is with the majesty of Omnipotence. Without Him, we are as sailing ships without a breeze, batteries without a spark, a sacrificial offering without the flame.

I am often made to feel this great lack to the humbling of my own spirit. You who teach in Sunday school or church, who witness for God among your friends and work mates, do you not feel your impotence and long for His power? Here is God's promise, "I will," given to those who are parched and dry. If we think ourselves to be well watered, if we are unconscious of deep need, then He pours nothing upon us.

It is upon the life that laments its barrenness and confesses its deadness that He delights to come. We just say to Him, "Lord, here is a bit of dry ground desperately in need of your life-giving water!" Then His Spirit comes in full measure.

Oh, that He would open the windows of heaven and send us a deluge of grace! Our sinful satisfaction with ourselves needs cleansing by the Spirit's abounding life and power. Let us plead this promise before the Throne: "Lord, have You not said You will pour water on the thirsty land? Then I present my dried-up life—do it for Your glory!"

The Lord gives a promise of revival, but what should we look for as the products of revival? Any work of God shows a marvelous stamp of authentic permanence. "They shall spring up like grass amid waters, like willows by flowing streams" (Isaiah 44:4 RSV). Wherever the living water comes, the grass will be sure to follow, and everything will come to life.

Wherever the Holy Spirit comes, there will be life in the church, renewal in the ministry, effectiveness in prayer, results in service, outstanding holiness, glowing love. All this leads to obviously converted lives: people who are clear in their testimony and complete in their surrender.

Charles Finney, the great preacher of the last century on revival, wrote as his definition of it:

> Renewal of the first love of Christians, resulting in the conversion of sinners to God. It presupposes that the church is backslidden, and revival means conviction of sin and searching of hearts among God's people. Revival is nothing less than a beginning of obedience to God—a breaking of heart and getting down into the dust before Him, with deep humility and forsaking of sin.
>
> A revival breaks that power of the world and of sin over Christians. The charm of the world is broken, and the power of sin is overcome. Truths to which our hearts are unresponsive suddenly become living. Whereas mind and conscience may assent to truth, when revival comes, obedience to the truth is the one thing that matters.

I would give my life to see that today! To hear, as Isaiah promised, "This one will say, 'I am the Lord's,' another will call himself by the name of Jacob, and another will write on his hand, 'The Lord's,' and surname himself by the name of Israel" (Isaiah 44:5 RSV). What a blessing to be branded with the name of our Maker! Oh, for such an outpouring of Holy Spirit power that we would see the tide turn in this poor, weary world!

I believe the course of history could be changed if the Christian church in the Western world would repent of its self-sufficient programs, its making of communism the main target of attack, while avoiding the priority need of facing its own sin. Dare *we* do that? Dare *I?* It has to begin with someone, so what about *you?* What about *me?* Imagine a circle, and put yourself in the middle, praying that God will renew by His Spirit everything within that circle.

John Wesley prayed, "Now, Lord, cure me of intermittent piety; make me consistent. Make my religion to be regular diet, not medicine to be taken when necessary. Don't let me go another moment in any sin of which I have not thoroughly repented."

God grant that this book, sent out for His glory, may be used to bring some into fullness of life in Christ, to be a flame of revival in the hand of God!